Albert Schweitzer

BOOKS BY JAMES BENTLEY

Ritualism and Politics in Victorian Britain:
The Attempt to Legislate for Belief
Between Marx and Christ:
The Dialogue in German-Speaking Europe, 1870–1970
Our Christian Heritage
Martin Niemöller
Oberammergau and the Passion Play
Secrets of Mount Sinai
Restless Bones: The Story of Relics
Cry God for England
A Children's Bible
A Calendar of Saints
The Life and Teaching of Jesus (with Audrey W. Bentley)
Christianity (with Audrey W. Bentley)
Contemporary Issues: A Christian View (with Audrey W. Bentley)
Mark (with Audrey W. Bentley)
Luke (with Audrey W. Bentley)
A Guide to the Dordogne
The Loire
The Languedoc
A Guide to Tuscany
West Germany and Berlin
Weekend Cities
Alsace
The Rhine
Normandy
Umbria
Bavaria
Italy: The Hilltowns
The Gateway to France

Albert Schweitzer

THE ENIGMA

James Bentley

HarperCollins*Publishers*

HarperCollins books may be purchased for educational, business, or sales promotional use. For information, please call or write: Special Markets Department, HarperCollins Publishers, Inc., 10 East 53rd Street, New York, NY 10022. Telephone: (212) 207-7528; Fax: (212) 207-7222.

FIRST EDITION

Designed by Alma Hochhauser Orenstein

Library of Congress Cataloging-in-Publication Data

Bentley, James, 1937–
    Albert Schweitzer : the enigma / James Bentley.—1st ed.
        p. cm.
    Includes bibliographical references and index.
    ISBN 0-06-016364-X
    1. Schweitzer, Albert, 1875–1965. 2. France—Biography.
3. Missionaries, Medical—Gabon—Biography. 4. Theologians—Europe—Biography. 5. Musicians—Europe—Biography. I. Title.
CT1018.S45B46   1992
610'.92—dc20
    [B]   91-50458

92 93 94 95 96 MAC/RRD 10 9 8 7 6 5 4 3 2

To Audrey W. Bentley

At Lambaréné I learned that a man does not have to be an angel to be a saint.

—NORMAN COUSINS

Contents

Acknowledgments

Every hitherto unpublished document quoted or cited in this book comes from the Albert Schweitzer Archive, 8 rue Münster, Gunsbach Village, 68140 Münster, Haut-Rhin, France. May I here express my gratitude to the Director and staff of the archive, who have given me much invaluable help.

Introduction

In a survey of West Germans carried out in 1985, out of thirty-two people dead or living, Albert Schweitzer topped the list as the most admired.

I find him an enigma, yet a man who never lost his ideals. He himself admitted that like most of us he was often tempted to do so: "We believed once in the victory of truth; but we do not now. We believed in our fellow men; but we do not now. We believed in goodness; but we do not now. We were zealous for justice; but we are not so now. We trusted in the power of kindness and peaceableness; we do not now. We were capable of enthusiasm; but we are not so now. To get through the shoals and storms of life more easily we have lightened our craft, throwing overboard what we thought could be spared. But it was really our stock of food and drink of which we deprived ourselves; our craft is now easier to manage, but we ourselves are in decline."

Since in the end he never abandoned his ideals, even when they were unpopular, his life remains a permanent inspiration.

In researching this book I have had the pleasure of meeting at Schweitzer's Gunsbach archive the late Ali Silver and her colleague Toni van Leer. I also owe an enormous debt to my wife, who researched the book with me and to whom it is gratefully dedicated.

CHAPTER 1

◆

A Tormented Childhood

lbert Schweitzer's celebrated cousin, the existentialist
philosopher Jean-Paul Sartre, began his memoir of his own
childhood—surely one of the bitterest ever published—
with a subtly vicious attack on Schweitzer's family. "In Alsace,
round about 1850," he wrote, "a clerical schoolmaster, burdened
with children, agreed to become a grocer. But he wanted some
compensation for unfrocking himself: since he had given up
forming minds, one of his sons would form souls; there would be
a pastor in the family, and it would be Charles." Charles, Sartre
continues, had other plans and ran away in pursuit of a female
circus rider. "His portrait was turned to the wall and all mention
of his name was forbidden." The sometime schoolmaster turned
to his second son, Auguste, and again was frustrated. To escape
ordination as a pastor, Auguste swiftly made the same sacrifice as
his father. He went into trade and prospered.

"That left Louis, who showed no special aptitude." According to Sartre, the father seized upon Louis and, before the placid
boy could make up his own mind, made a pastor of him. "Then
Louis carried obedience a stage further by himself begetting a
minister, Albert Schweitzer, whose career is well known."

Schweitzer himself told a different story. In 1875, the year of
Albert Schweitzer's birth, his father, Louis-Théophile, was serv-

ing as Protestant pastor of Kaysersberg in Alsace. "A few weeks after I was born," wrote Albert Schweitzer in 1931, "my father moved to Gunsbach in the Münster Valley. There with my three sisters and one brother I experienced an extremely happy childhood, troubled only by the frequent illnesses of my father." "Later," Schweitzer continued, "his health improved. As a sturdy septuagenarian he cared for his flock during the [First World] War, when the French artillery fire raked the valley from the heights of the Vosges mountains, claiming as victims many a house and native of Gunsbach. He died at a great age in 1925."

Albert Schweitzer began his own account of his childhood and youth in an almost coldly factual fasion. "I was born in the little town of Kaysersberg, in Upper Alsace, on January 14, 1875, in the small house with the turret which you see on the left as you leave the upper end of the town." No hint of the possible frustrations of his parents and grandparents is allowed to creep into his narrative. "My paternal grandfather was the schoolmaster and organist at Pfaffenhofen in Lower Alsace, and three of his brothers had similar posts," he continues. "My mother Adèle (born a Schillinger) was the daughter of a Pastor of Mühlbach in the Münster Valley in Upper Alsace."

Even though Kaysersberg was savagely bombed in the Second World War, Schweitzer's birthplace still stands, a handsome half-timbered house with dormer windows, an archway leading into its courtyard, and a little tower rising from the roof. Such was the substantial home of Louis-Théophile Schweitzer, Lutheran pastor of Kaysersberg. Albert was his second child, following a daughter, Louisa, one year later.

Kaysersberg, the "mount of Caesar," takes its name from the nearby hill on which the Romans built a fort to control a route across the mountains into Gaul. Down the years this route remained important, and so the town prospered. In the thirteenth century the Emperor Frederick II built a castle, virtually on the site of the Roman fort. Its ruins still stand. Happily, after World War II almost every war-damaged building in Kaysersberg was meticulously restored, so that today the exquisite little town looks much as it did on the day Albert Schweitzer was born.

For the young pastor's son, the old houses and streets of Kaysersberg were redolent of a different kind of history. It was a matter of pride for Schweitzer that it was from Kaysersberg that Geiler von Kaysersberg, the famous medieval preacher, took his surname. Born at Schaffhausen in Switzerland, Geiler was brought up in Kaysersberg after his father's death by his grandfather. He made his name as a preacher in Strasbourg Cathedral in the years immediately preceding the Reformation, and died in 1510, just before the immense split in western Christendom between Catholic and Protestant occurred. That the Protestant Albert Schweitzer could so revere one who lived and died a Catholic tells us something about the unusual religious complexion of late-nineteenth-century Alsace, as well as sheds light upon Schweitzer's own temperament.

Alsace lies on the borders of Germany and France and is probably most generally known for its distinctive wines. Schweitzer was to confess himself delighted to have been born in the year of an unusually fine Alsatian vintage. While climate and soil have blessed the province, it has suffered dreadfully as a battleground—especially during the Wars of Religion in the sixteenth century and during the Thirty Years' War in the next. In both conflicts Catholics and Protestants cruelly slaughtered each other, their miseries compounded by famine and plague. Nowhere did these conflicts rage more fiercely than in the land of Albert Schweitzer's birth, the midpoint between Protestant Germany and Catholic France.

Curiously enough, the result was that in Alsace there arose a degree of religious toleration found scarcely anywhere else in Christendom. The late-sixteenth-century Edict of Nantes had decreed a measure of religious toleration between Catholics and Protestants. In the next century the ruler of Alsace, King Louis XIV of France, determined to revoke the Edict, suppressing Protestant freedom of worship. But he was not totally master of Alsace. Cantons, towns, and cities of the province had voluntarily accepted his suzerainty without surrendering all their ancient liberties. Protestants in particular were determined to hold onto their old religious freedoms. To protect the rights of Catholics, Louis XIV insisted on a unique compromise. He decreed that in Alsace wherever a parish comprised a minority of at least seven Catholics, these Christians should have the right to worship in the chancel of the Protestant church and occupy the whole building for certain hours on Sunday. So here Protestants and Catholics had learned to live at peace and to cooperate with one another.

In Kaysersberg, where Protestants were in the minority, Albert Schweitzer's father taught Lutheran Christianity to a tiny congregation set amidst a majority of Catholics. When he became pastor of predominantly Protestant Gunsbach a year after Albert's birth, Catholicism, as a result of Louis XIV's decree, still had a presence in the town. For Louis-Théophile, and later for his son Albert Schweitzer (as for most Alsatians), this was no burden. Quite the contrary: To Albert's youthful gaze the Catholic chancel of Gunsbach Church was "the *ne plus ultra* of magnificence. There was first an altar painted to look like gold, with huge branches of artificial flowers upon it; then tall candlesticks of metal with majestic wax candles in them; on the wall, above the altar and between the two windows, was a pair of large gilt statues, which to me were Joseph and the Virgin Mary; and all these objects were flooded with the light which came through the chancel windows."

Albert Schweitzer was to become for a time a severely rationalist theologian. Yet the entrancing Catholic chancel at Gunsbach never ceased to be part of a lifelong romantic dream—a diffused fantasy that was by no means specifically religious. Through the stained-glass window he gazed in his imagination upon "trees, roofs, clouds, and blue sky," upon a world "in short, which continued the chancel of the church into an infinity of distance, and was, in its turn, flooded with a kind of transfiguring glory imparted to it by the chancel." The young boy desperately needed such dreams. He was for the most part deeply miserable as we shall see. As he put it, his gaze, wandering from the finite to the infinite, enabled his soul to be "wrapped in peace and quiet."

At various times in his life Schweitzer was to make decisions that defy explanation. From time to time a romantic irrationalism would subdue his almost clinical, even arrogant intelligence. His preference for Catholic emotion as opposed to cool Protestant clarity is an example. He despaired when Protestant architects designed churches in such a way that the pulpit—the potent symbol and the very setting of preaching—was elevated above all else. To preach is to appeal to the mind rather than the heart. "When I see churches in which modern architects have tried to embody the ideal of 'a preacher's church,' I feel a sinking at the heart," Schweitzer confessed. "A church is much more than a building in which one listens to sermons; it is a place for devotions, and merely as a building it ought to keep people at a devotional level." Albert Schweitzer resented the fact that some years later an "art-loving priest from Münster" had replaced the magnificent gilded altar at Gunsbach with a Modernistic piece, relegating the Virgin Mary to one side wall and Saint Joseph to another. No longer did they seem to bless the whole church and its congregation; they simply stared at each other. Moreover, the Virgin's glittering gilt had been stripped away and replaced with a dress of blue, red, and green.

Still, whenever he returned home Albert Schweitzer would go into the church, close his eyes, and summon up a vision of its long-lost decor and, with it, the ghosts of long-dead worshippers as they sat there solemnly, the men in sober black, the women in their simple Münster Valley costume. Others too in Gunsbach Church experienced this identification with those Christians whom they believed had left this world for a better one. For these worshippers, far more important than the views of a nineteenth-century preacher was their sense of unity with the saints of old, as well as with the Christians of their own day. Schweitzer watched, listened to, and learned from these men and women. He remembered an old man called Mitschi, so deaf that he could hear not a word of the sermon. Once his father had gone so far as to let Mitschi know how much he regretted that the deaf old man was obliged to worship without hearing a word of what was said (in particular, Louis Schweitzer's sermons). Mitschi "shook his head with a smile and said: 'The Communion of Saints, Herr Pfarrer, the Communion of Saints!'"

Does Schweitzer tell this story almost as a criticism of his father? Louis Schweitzer was steeped in the Lutheran tradition of earnest, dedicated preaching, and Albert must have heard hundreds of his sermons. He was to write repeatedly, in several memoirs, of the apparent perfection of his home life as a child, while continually dropping hints that all might not have been well. Unlike Sartre, Albert Schweitzer was never known to have made the slightest unkind reference to his father, to his uncles on his father's side, or to his paternal grandfather. If Sartre's candor may be called uncharitable, how do we interpret Schweitzer's apparent reverence toward his father's family? Was it simply an act of filial piety, or was it also a device to conceal from the world his own inner anxieties and what may even have been the traumas of his youth? The answer to such questions is hard to find. Time and again the true nature of the man is obscured as if by a smoke screen.

Yet Schweitzer published widely, and his private papers were carefully preserved throughout his long life, as they are today in the archive at Gunsbach. The plain fact seems to be that Schweitzer threw up the smoke screen himself. His published autobiographical writings, when compared with one another in the context of his archive, can be perceived as designed to present a face to the world that would be consistent with the image that the world came to have of him. Yet by reading between the lines it is possible to establish that the great man's childhood and youth were by no means so idyllic as he suggested.

When Schweitzer wrote—and spoke—about his childhood, he dwelt on the historical significance of his birthplace rather than face the profound problems that beset his family. Even so, in 1922 he did confess some of his youthful traumas to his friend the Swiss psychiatrist and Protestant clergyman Oscar Pfister. Though Pfister was a friend, it was a formal consultation.

Schweitzer wrote out an account of his life, and Pfister annotated it.

The analysis took place after his internment by the French during World War I, when Schweitzer was plunged into a severe depression that Pfister helped to cure. But so cleverly did Albert Schweitzer conceal the traumas of his early emotional life that this central episode in his development has never been allowed to surface. His published writings cleverly minimize the significance of his analysis by Pfister in his return to sanity. In one account Schweitzer even gets wrong the date of his analysis, assigning his meeting with Pfister to 1923, instead of 1922. In later life he vigorously tried to conceal the very fact that he had suffered any kind of nervous breakdown.

James Brabazon, an acute biographer, was completely misled by Schweitzer's emotional duplicity on this point. Writing in 1975, Brabazon naively declared:

> Pfister persuaded him to speak of his early memories, and the result was *Memoirs of My Childhood and Youth*. This was the meeting which George Marshall, in his recent biography, quotes as additional evidence that Schweitzer after the war suffered "a nervous breakdown." In fact by this time Schweitzer had been back on the top of his form for nearly three years—and there is a small epilogue to the story which clinches the matter. When, years later, Schweitzer damaged his hand and was taken by Erica Anderson to a Zürich doctor to have it attended to, the doctor's nurse turned out to be Oscar Pfister's daughter. She remembered the occasion well as a cheerful social visit and nothing more. The truth is the worst thing that Schweitzer suffered from at this period was an attack of *otitis media*, or inflammation of the middle ear.

Schweitzer himself wrote that he merely spent two or three hours with his friend, who soothed his anguish. The weight of suppression here is indeed heavy.

In none of Schweitzer's published writings is his analysis ever mentioned. In the Schweitzer archive at Gunsbach are to be found not one but several letters in which Albert Schweitzer urgently begs Oscar Pfister to send back to his patient the crucial self-analysis. The annotated document was returned, remains in the archive, and is extraordinarily revealing. The dreadful word in Schweitzer's whole self-analysis is "tortured."

This is not to say that in his autobiographical writings he did not speak sincerely, simply that what he wrote fails to tell the whole truth. Yet glimpses appear. Even when he was striving to eliminate all elements of criticism directed at his home life and parents, Schweitzer expresses his doubts as to whether the idyll he is portraying is not somehow contrary to what a true Christian ought to expect. "When I consider my early life I am moved by thinking of the very many people whom I have to thank for what they gave me or were to me," he wrote. "The thought that I had been granted such a specially happy youth was ever in my mind." Yet, he said, later he began to question this right to happiness. "Out of the depths of my feeling of happiness there gradually arose inside me an understanding of Jesus's saying that we must not regard our lives as belonging to ourselves alone."

In truth Albert Schweitzer never totally reconciled his desire for happiness and even acclaim with the guilt and reticence he here expresses. Schweitzer was a split personality as a child and remained similarly torn for the rest of his life. In his long adult years he was to cherish his own family and yet spend months away from them. He devoted himself to black men and women, and was passionately opposed to racism; yet at Lambaréné he supervised a hierarchical missionary hospital in which only whites held positions of responsibility. He despairingly rejected Western civilization; yet he continually returned to it. He would sometimes turn away from Christianity to the religions of India; yet he remained fascinated by Jesus, Saint Paul, and Christian mysticism. If our formative infant years dominate the rest of our lives, then the clues offered by Albert Schweitzer's early life are crucial to an understanding of his later outstanding career, as well as to his influence on and contribution to the spiritual and intellectual heritage of our own century. There is a constant turbulence underlying his life. He underwent sudden conversions, transforming his pattern of life and thought at whatever cost to himself and those around him. He learned to cope and survive with his own contradictions.

This pattern started early in his life. His family's move from lovely Kaysersberg to the far less attractive Gunsbach took place when Albert was six months old. The child was so ill at the time that at one point his parents thought he had died, but milk from a neighbor's cow revived him. On the occasion of Louis Schweitzer's induction as pastor of his new church, his wife decked their sick child in a white dress decorated with colored ribbons, hoping that the wives of the pastors taking part in the ceremony would delight in her new baby. Sadly they did not, and she was later to tell her son again and again that not a single one could bring herself to compliment her on the thin, yellow-faced infant. They were too embarrassed to find the words. As they stammered out commonplace remarks, the distraught mother took up her child in her arms and fled to her bedroom, weeping hot tears over him.

Soon he recovered, and Louis and Adèle Schweitzer gave birth to four more children. One daughter named Emma died young, so that Albert was brought up alongside three sisters and one brother. Gunsbach brought him security, so much so that when he won the Goethe Prize in 1928 he used the money to build a permanent home there, a square, solid, rather ugly house facing toward the mountains.

Yet Gunsbach also held terrors for the young Schweitzer, and above all inside his father's church. The young Albert was allowed (not forced) to attend services there as soon as he was three or four years old. He was entranced, enthusiastic, even occasionally bored. When he sang too loudly or yawned, a maid's cotton glove would suddenly cover his lips. Then he would see the devil. Albert's Satan was the organist, a bearded, shaggy individual who would peer into the body of the church by means of a looking glass whenever he was accompanying the congregation's singing. Young Albert spotted his distorted visage in the mirror and was consumed with fear. As soon as Pastor Louis began to preach, the devil would vanish. Albert

Schweitzer, trying to make sense of this terrifying mystery, concluded that Satan cannot abide a sermon: "As soon as father begins God's Word, he has to make himself scarce."

The young Schweitzer also was burdened with guilt. Still wearing skirts, he was sitting on a stool close to his father's beehives while Louis worked with the bees. Suddenly a bee settled on the boy and began crawling about on his hand. Albert was at first delighted, but when the bee stung him he began to shriek in terror and pain. Instantly he was the center of attention. The maidservant hugged and kissed him. His mother rounded on Louis for working at the hives without first making sure that their son was safe. Albert was so delighted with this attention that he continued to cry long after the pain had disappeared. Being an introverted child, it was not long before he realized what he was doing. His conscience told him to stop weeping, but he was so gratified at being the center of attention that he kept up the charade. By the time the incident was over, Albert was desolated by his own duplicity and miserable for the rest of the day. His own later comment was: "How often in after life, when assailed by temptation, has this experience warned me against exaggerating, or making too much of, whatever has happened to me!"

Because of his recurrent need to exorcise the demons of anxiety and to come to terms with his own personality, a personality created in part by a tormented childhood, Schweitzer suffered a nervous breakdown, sought psychiatric help, and wrote and rewrote memoirs of his life that both conceal and reveal his inner life. Incident after incident in Schweitzer's memoirs of his youth is filled with moral trauma, with anxiety, even with terror. The church sacristan and gravedigger, Jägle, was, he wrote, "the terror of my childhood," persuading the boy that he was growing horns on his head. Did Jägle spot Albert's powerful anxieties and morbid imagination, thus managing to convince the boy that demonic horns really were sprouting from him?

Albert also dreaded Christmas because of the impossible task of writing thank-you letters for his presents. "For years I used to salt with my tears the meals between Christmas and the

New Year, and once I began to cry on Christmas Day itself, directly after the distribution of the presents, at the thought of the inevitable letters which would have to be written!" For the rest of his life Albert Schweitzer forbade nephews, nieces, and godchildren to write a letter of thanks after receiving one of his presents.

There was a deeper passion also. As a child Albert Schweitzer had longed to win at everything, so that to play a game with him was a terrifying experience. It was terrifying if he lost, and it was terrifying if he won, for the boy despised an easy victory and would often fly into a rage if one were offered to him. This violence in his nature disturbed him deeply, and once again such incidents were formative for his adult life. "From that time onwards I began to feel anxious about my passion for play," he recalled, "and gradually gave up all games."

One of Albert's youthful attempts to cope with stress of this kind was to identify strongly with two of his ancestors, to try to incorporate, as it were, their virtues by making them his own. He was proud that his mother was born a Schillinger, "the daughter of the distinguished pastor of Mühlbach in the Münster Valley." Johann Jakob Schillinger, his maternal grandfather, was undoubtedly the most distinguished of his ancestors. Pastor at Mühlbach from 1829 until his death in 1872, he had first married Marie-Salomé Graff, who bore him a son, baptized Charles-Albert. After she died in 1829 Pastor Schillinger married his second wife, Caroline Kessel, who bore him Adèle, Albert Schweitzer's mother. Schweitzer relished the tales told about his maternal grandfather: when there was some special astronomical phenomenon to be observed, how he would set up his telescope in front of his house so that anyone interested could peer through it; how, after a church service, he used to recount to his parishioners Europe's latest political and intellectual developments; how he prepared his sermons with the utmost care; how merrily he would carve—or slice into sections—the traditional Münster Valley meat pie at weddings and baptisms. Pastor Schillinger was a man of God, yet one inexorably drawn to the eighteenth-century Enlightenment. Happily, the Catholic priest who also officiated in Schillinger's parish was similarly obsessed. Pastor Schillinger and he lived, Schweitzer tells us, in brotherly union. When the Catholic priest was on holiday, Pastor Schillinger took care of his colleague's parishioners and vice versa. If one parsonage was too small, each gave hospitality to the other's visitors.

On his father's side Schweitzer's ancestry, a long line of schoolmasters, schoolmistresses, and clergymen stretching back at least as far as the seventeenth century, was equally impressive. Although the name Schweitzer clearly indicates a Swiss root in Albert's family tree, his first Alsatian ancestor, Johann Nikolaus Schweitzer, was the son of a shipbuilder (also named Johann) of Frankfurt am Main. In 1662 at Strasbourg he married Maria Elizabeth Hermann, daughter of a master of the mint. His second wife, whom he married in 1672, was a lawyer's daughter named Barbara Oesinger. Johann Nikolaus Schweitzer became a Protestant pastor in Kork, in Westhofen, and in Strasbourg, where he died in 1675.

His successors included Johann Jakob Schweitzer, who was a teacher at Boofzheim, as also was his son Johann Louis. To add to this pedagogic pedigree, Albert Schweitzer's great-grandfather, Johann Christian, himself schoolmaster at Eckwer-sheim, begat eleven children, of which no fewer than seven also became schoolteachers. One son, Philipp Christian, followed his father's footsteps and became the schoolmaster at Pfaffenhofen, where he met his wife, Catherine Heyt. An ardent republican, he refused to swear the oath of loyalty to Napoleon III, was forced to renounce his profession, and became a grocer. Between 1875 and 1886 this admirable Philipp Christian was mayor of Pfaffen-hofen. This was the Philipp Christian toward whom Jean-Paul Sartre was merciless. The mayor's sons, also mocked by Sartre, were Auguste (who made his fortune in exports and imports in Paris); Charles (who became a teacher in Paris at the Lycée Louis-le-Grand); and Albert Schweitzer's own father, Louis-Théophile.

Albert also identified with another forebear, though more somberly. This was his mother's half brother, Charles-Albert, after whom he had been named. Albert Schillinger had been pastor of the Church of Saint-Nicolas, Strasbourg. There, during the Franco-Prussian War of 1870–71, he had performed an heroic act for which he was to be cruelly reviled. After the Battle of Weissenburg in 1870 Albert Schillinger had set off to Paris to find drugs and medicaments for the city of Strasbourg, which was soon to be besieged by German troops. No one could have made the journey in time. By the time the pastor returned to his cure of souls, Strasbourg was suffering an unprecedentedly savage bombardment by the enemy. The besieging commander, General von Werder, allowed the medical supplies through but kept Pastor Albert prisoner. Schweitzer continues the story: "He thus had to live through the siege among the besiegers, tormented by the thought that his flock might be thinking that in that difficult time he had of his own accord left them in the lurch." Albert Schillinger had a weak heart, and the results of all the turmoil of these months were too much for him. In the summer of 1872, while standing with a group of friends in Strasbourg, he fell to the ground dead.

Baptized in the name of this tragic figure, Schweitzer did not merely recount this story as some pitiful tale. Instead, he personally felt the need to fulfill the potential of Pastor Albert Schillinger's truncated life. This impulse of Schweitzer's was exacerbated by the knowledge that his mother had adored her dead half-brother. Continually she repeated to her son tales illustrating her dead hero's virtues. Young Albert was competing with and setting himself alongside a paragon of virtue whom he had never met, who could never again be found wanting. It was an impossibly tormenting task. "The thought of how I could provide, as it were, a continuation of a man whom my mother had loved so much haunted me a great deal, especially as I had heard so many stories of his kindness," he wrote. "When after the siege of Strasbourg there was for a time a shortage of milk, he used to bring his allowance to a poor old woman who after his death told my mother how, during that period, she had got her daily milk."

Identifying at one remove with his mother, yet identifying

with two pastors instead of his father, the young Albert was a bundle of emotional contradictions. As he remembered, his mother, whose half-brother he longed to reincarnate, was frequently in tears. Yet from her he learned a means of release from his tensions: the countryside. "Here," she would say, as they walked by a much-loved lakeside, "I am completely at home. Here among the rocks, among the woods. I came here as a child. Let me breathe the fragrance of the fir trees and enjoy the quiet of this refuge from the world. Do not speak. After I am no longer on earth, come here and think of me."

When he recounted this, Schweitzer was forty years old. How far was he enhancing the truth and presenting an idealized vision of a much less romantic reality? The acerbic Jean-Paul Sartre certainly believed Schweitzer did so. He had picked up reminiscences of Albert's father and his two brothers that showed them in a totally different light: telling scatological stories to each other; scandalizing the ladies until they feigned migraines, retiring to bed, hating the "noise, passion and enthusiasm, all the shabby vulgarity of life with the Schweitzers." These Schweitzer menfolk were, wrote Sartre, "creatures of nature and puritans—a combination of virtues less rare than people think." The Schweitzers, he added, "loved coarse words which, while they minimized the body in true Christian fashion, manifested their willing acceptance of the natural functions."

Sartre's grandfather would from time to time visit the pastor's household in Gunsbach and create havoc. When staying at Gunsbach, Sartre remembered, "Charles never failed to rail against his sister-in-law; several times a week, he would fling his napkin down on the table and leave the dining-room, slamming the door;... After meals we would go and weep and moan at his feet and he would respond with a haughty look." Yet none of this turmoil was ever mentioned by Albert Schweitzer. He had suppressed it all. In public Albert Schweitzer and Jean-Paul Sartre remained cordial, amicable, perfectly correct. In the year that Jean-Paul Sartre's memoir was published, he wrote to Albert Schweitzer, his "Dear Uncle Albert." His letter ends, "Will you please allow me most affectionately to embrace you?"

As some might understandably have done, Schweitzer did not reply with venom. His letter in response to Sartre's contains not a word of rebuke.

It is clear that Albert Schweitzer was driven by conflicting desires: to reveal himself and to hide. To publish two memoirs of his childhood and youth displays either great vanity or (what in this case appears to be the truth) an overwhelming need to explore himself. He was after all an unblinking Christian and a searcher after truth. Yet some aspects of his life were too painful either for him to look at or to allow others to contemplate. His amiable relations with Jean-Paul Sartre, in spite of Sartre's savage attack on the Gunsbach home, indicate a desire not to follow the furrow Sartre was ploughing, above all not to examine too painfully his own profoundly influential formative relationships with his parents. Albert Schweitzer admits in his autobiographical writings some anxieties about his father's health, and the family's consequent fear of destitution. Almost immediately he blithely sweeps these anxieties away. "As time went on we were saved from the worst of our money worries," he wrote, "for a distant relative of my mother's, who had no children, left us her small fortune, and during my last years at school there was again unclouded sunshine in my home."

With regard to his parents, and especially to his mother, Schweitzer on the psychiatrist's couch revealed tremendous angst:

> "When I was aged between seven and eight, my father became very ill," he said. "Then, for the first time, I came to know the anxieties that had flowed through our household for many years: financial anxieties, anxieties about health. Then my mother honestly said to me, if my father died, she and the five children (of whom I was the second) would certainly be flung out of the house. This thought tortured me, because I thought then we should be without doubt destitute."

Dreading destitution and seeing his mother practicing all sorts of economies, the young boy began to take a pride in making his own wants as small as possible. Once his mother suggested that he needed a new winter suit. Albert protested that his present suit was perfectly adequate. Since it was unusable, he was obliged to attend school in his summer suit. The ridicule he received from his fellow pupils he regarded as readily endurable if it lessened his mother's anxieties.

Thus underlying Albert Schweitzer's childhood and youth was a deep, pervasive insecurity. Yet as far as he could he kept it all to himself. In spite of his public position and enormous fame, Schweitzer remained throughout his life a secretive, self-protecting man. In a passage whose passionate conviction is revealing, he once wrote, "I believe that no-one should force himself to show to others more of his inner life than he feels it natural to reveal." Schweitzer half-admitted that this passionately held insight derived from his own fight to protect his inner self as a child. "It was perhaps a result of my inherited reserve that from my youth up reverence for the personalities of others became to me something natural and a matter of course. Since then I have become more and more confirmed in this view through seeing how much sorrow, pain and mutual estrangement come from people claiming the right to read the souls of others as they might read one of the books they own."

So, although he felt close to his mother, they never put their mutual love into words. As Schweitzer explained it, "We did not possess the faculty of verbally expressing the affection we had for each other, and I can count on my fingers the hours in which we really talked to each other heart to heart. But," he added, "we understood each other without putting it into words." When she was suddenly and accidentally killed, trampled under the horses of cavalrymen in 1916, he bottled up the effect on himself. Having described in his memoirs his father's ripe old age, almost as an afterthought, Schweitzer baldly adds, "My mother was knocked down and killed in 1916 by cavalry horses on the road between Gunsbach and Weier-in-Tal." There is nothing else: no comment, no emotion.

"My father was my dearest friend," he wrote. But again Schweitzer's own published memoirs, read closely, also reveal a far more somber relationship and one that he later did not much like to acknowledge. At times hints appear. "Even to-day,"

Schweitzer confessed in his forties, "I do not feel quite comfortable in my father's study." His conscious explanation for this involved the dreaded Christmas chore of writing thank-you letters for their Christmas presents. Albert and his sisters did this in the pastor's study. Louisa possessed the enviable knack of making each letter slightly different, even though each letter said much the same thing. Albert would take hours to write even one. Then the letter had to be submitted to his father, corrected and criticized, and rewritten in an improved form, without a blot. As we have seen, for many years the boy would cry over his meals between Christmas and the New Year, and he once began to weep the moment the presents had been handed round on Christmas Day itself, overwhelmed by the thought of the miserable task that lay ahead.

Yet this alone cannot explain why the adult Albert Schweitzer always felt such anxiety whenever he visited his dead father's study in Gunsbach. Schweitzer himself suggests that the reasons went deeper. He confessed that he had never as child set foot inside his father's study unless he was absolutely compelled to do so. By his own account, this loathing was not solely the result of the hateful chore of writing the Christmas thank-you letters. It also involved an element of rejecting Pastor Louis.

For Louis Schweitzer possessed considerable literary and theological talents of his own. Taking his cue from a Swiss pastor named Jeremiah Gotthelf, Louis-Théophile Schweitzer wrote charming little village tales, stories of the peasant happenings in his own home country (the region of Hanau), as well as those in the Münster Valley. He published these stories in the local *Church Messenger* (the *Elsass-lothringischer Familienkalender*) between 1895 and 1909. Watching his father studying and writing amid an all-pervasive smell of books, young Albert found the whole scene "terribly unnatural."

Pastor Louis-Théophile Schweitzer was no dunce. Educated (as his son would be) at the University of Strasbourg, he had there completed a fine thesis on the theologian Johannes Mathesius. For a pastor and preacher of Louis-Théophile's temperament, the subject was ideal. Johannes Mathesius had been one of the most noted and powerful preachers of the Reformation. After an education at the University of Wittenberg, Johannes in 1532 was appointed rector of the Latin school at Joachimstal in northwestern Bohemia. Eight years later he returned to Wittenberg and became a table companion of Martin Luther himself, making notes of the great reformer's table talk. Two years later Luther ordained him.

Mathesius was Martin Luther's first biographer, publishing at Nuremberg in 1566 a celebrated and devoted account of the Reformer's life. But his chief claim to glory consisted of twenty-five years devoted to preaching and the cure of souls in the church at Joachimstal. Distracted by the need to appeal at Prague before King Ferdinand I in defense of Protestants during the Schmalkaldic War, rejecting an invitation to become a professor at the University of Leipzig, worn out by persecution and religious wars, Johannes Mathesius labored on, producing lives of the Protestant saints as a counterpoint to the traditional Catholic homilies on Catholic saints, and above all preaching and publishing humorous, blunt, and gentle sermons.

Schweitzer's father warmed above all to Mathesius's preaching. His sermons were widely circulated and translated. During Carnival time, when even a pastor was meant to unbend, Mathesius preached some exceedingly witty homilies addressed to those who mined silver, the industry that had made Protestant Northwestern Bohemia so prosperous. After his early death, at only sixty-one, he became revered there as "the angel of the church." Johannes Mathesius was Louis-Théophile Schweitzer's ideal clergyman.

Faced with all this, his son Albert went so far as to vow never to become a student, preacher, or writer, for this was what his father was. Later the scholar tried to modify this immature judgment, admiring the charm of his father's village tales. He insisted that his father was stern with the children only when they were writing their Christmas thank-you letters—transformed into the soul of kindness and understanding for the rest of the year. But Louis Schweitzer's study remained for his son "a most uncomfortable place."

If in later life Albert Schweitzer liked to dub his father his own dearest friend, in truth, their relations were in part poisoned (a word used by Albert Schweitzer himself) by the conflict between the impoverished but genteel clerical home and the pull of the normal life of Gunsbach, where Albert first met the outside world. The child of Pastor Louis Schweitzer would wear only fingerless gloves, since the village boys possessed no others. On weekdays he refused to wear shoes out of doors, for village boys wore only clogs, saving their leather boots for Sundays. Yet Louis Schweitzer demanded that his son dress "suitably for his station in life," repeatedly boxing his ears, beating him, and shutting him in the cellar when the boy refused to wear a new jacket.

Indoors Albert gave way. Outdoors he refused. As he put it, "I stood firm," as if some enormous principle were involved. Throughout these conflicts Albert regarded himself as "a courageous hero." Inwardly, he hated his conformity inside the walls of the parsonage. The rich soup on his family table was nauseating to him, since the boys he competed with in the village taunted him because they ate worse than he did.

It was, he recalled, "a real grief to me to be so perverse with my parents." Only his sister Louisa had some inkling of why he felt like this and showed a measure of sympathy. Alas for the harmony of the family and the psychological development of Albert Schweitzer, "This stern contest" (to use his own words again) "lasted all the time that I was at the village school," poisoning "not only my life but that of my father too."

Schweitzer described himself as a "sprig of the gentry," and he hated the role—undoubtedly one of the reasons for his later identification with the outcasts of the world. Eventually he and Louis Schweitzer gained a measure of mutual tolerance, and a feeling of mutual peace grew up between them. Typically, Schweitzer was humble enough to accept responsibility for many of the troubles that had arisen between them. "Never, after I had abandoned my unfortunate disputatiousness," he wrote, "was there in our home any more tension between the father and his grown-up son."

CHAPTER 2

♦

Unwillingly to School

I did not look forward to going to school," Albert Schweitzer recalled. "When on a fine October day my father for the first time put a slate under my arm and led me away to the schoolmistress, I cried the whole way there." The young lad suspected, rightly, that his dreaming and much of his glorious freedom were coming to an end.

But he found no trouble in learning to read and write. And there were other compensations peculiar to Albert's strange, remarkably observant temperament. One was the visit of a school inspector named Steinart. When Inspector Steinart arrived, the young Schweitzer noted with interest the trembling hands of the schoolmistress and the fawning behavior of the village organist, who also doubled as a schoolmaster. Far from being terrified himself, the boy was enthralled, for Steinart was the first man he had ever set eyes on who had written a book— or rather two books, the green one used to teach the middle school and the yellow one of the upper standard. To Schweitzer these textbooks ranked only beneath the Bible itself. To be sure, Steinart was not outwardly prepossessing. "His exterior was not imposing; he was small, bald-headed, red-nosed, had a big stomach, and was enveloped in a grey suit, but to my eyes he had a halo round him, for he was a man who had written a book." For the schoolmistress and the church organist to talk with him, just as they were able to talk to any other mortal, seemed to young Albert incomprehensible.

There are the contradictions of childhood here—though of an intensely bookish childhood. Albert Schweitzer had decided in his conscious mind that in no way would he follow his father's pattern and be a pastor who sat writing in a musty, book-lined study. Yet he simultaneously exulted at the sight of his first real-life author.

At school he suffered a humiliation, a betrayal, the effects of which were still strong forty years later. A new teacher named Fräulein Goguel arrived. As with all new teachers, she needed time to win her pupils' approval. Before Albert Schweitzer had properly accepted her, he decided that she must be a "cripple." Fräulein Goguel was in fact a perfectly healthy woman; the young Schweitzer did not know what the word meant. "Cripple," for his youthful mind, simply indicated some strong dissatisfaction. Dissatisfied with Fräulein Goguel, he declared her a cripple.

He made the mistake of confiding this secret to his dearest school friend when they were both looking after cows. His friend promised not to tell anyone. Shortly afterward he and Albert had a quarrel on the way to school. On the school steps Albert's friend threatened to tell the new teacher precisely how her wayward pupil described her. Schweitzer was certain that the threat would never be carried out, but when break came his erstwhile friend went up to the teacher's desk and announced, "Fräulein, Albert has called you a cripple." Happily, Miss Goguel had no idea what the false friend was talking about. Albert was not punished. What remained was a permanent wound: the knowledge that even a friend can betray. "This first experience of treachery shattered to atoms all that I had thought or expected of life," he wrote. It was weeks before he recovered from the shock. "Of the blows that I have received since then," he later confessed, "many have been harder, but there has not been one so painful."

Painful is the mot juste for describing Albert Schweitzer's

relationships with his companions in these early years. A friendly tussle would turn into a deeply mortifying experience, even—
or especially—when Schweitzer won. Deeply shy and reserved,
he longed for acceptance by the other village boys. For their part,
he could never escape from his role as a pastor's son and thus
one of the gentry, inevitably set apart from them. He once wres-
tled with a bigger boy named George Nitschelm. George should
have won, but Albert put him down, at which the vanquished
boy remarked, "If I got broth to eat twice a week, as you do, I
should be as strong as you." Schweitzer was mortified. He grew
to hate the broth which steamed twice weekly on the semi-
impoverished table of his own home.

His parents, particularly his father, found equally painful
this rejection of their valiant attempts to feed and clothe their
son properly. Unable to afford a new overcoat for Albert, they
had the tailor fashion one for him out of an old overcoat of Pastor Louis. As the tailor began to fit it, he made the innocent,
though in this case injudicious remark, "Albert, now you're a
regular gentleman." It was enough to make the boy refuse ever
to wear this refurbished handed-down garment, for no other village child possessed an overcoat. The first time he refused to put
it on was for church one Sunday. Pastor Louis boxed his ears, to
no avail. Again and again Albert's ears were boxed, but never
would he wear that overcoat.

Another time the boy was taken by his mother to Strasbourg, where an elderly relative offered to buy him a new cap.
The shop assistant brought out a handsome-looking sailor's cap;
but no other boy in Gunsbach wore such a cap, and Albert
adamantly turned it down. Eventually the infuriated shop assistant shouted, "What sort of cap do you want, you stupid lad?"
Albert replied, "I'll have one like what the village boys wear." A
shop girl was sent to find among unsalable stock a brown cap
that could be pulled down over a boy's ears. Beaming, Albert
screwed it down on his head. He knew that his dignified mother
felt shamed before the cultivated citizens of Strasbourg. But,
unlike her husband, in spite of this shame she allowed no word
of reproach to her son to pass her lips.

A profound, complex inner torment in Albert was the result. At odds with his parents because of his desire to identify with the other children of Gunsbach, Albert Schweitzer could nonetheless never be one of them. He alone, in school photographs, wears an immaculately starched collar among the homely, ungainly clothing of the rest of the class. George Nitschelm had put into his own words what Albert Schweitzer already felt to be true: "The village boys did not accept me as one of themselves."

He was not one of them. Consciously, at times, he felt himself turning against their ways. They used to mock a man named Mausche, a Jewish cattle and land dealer, whenever he arrived from a nearby village on his donkey cart. Inevitably in those anti-Semitic times, Mausche was reckoned to be a usurer and a property jobber. In addition, he was the only Jew anyone had ever seen, and the Gunsbach boys would run after his cart, folding the corners of their shirts or jackets to look like pigs' ears and crying "Mausche, Mausche." Albert felt he could not be considered grown up if he did not join in. But Mausche was his match, in a remarkable way. With his freckles and gray beard he drove on out of the village as far as the bridge, as unperturbed as his donkey, save that several times he turned round and looked at them all with an embarrassed but good-natured smile. "This smile overpowered me," Albert Schweitzer remembered. Thenceforth, instead of running behind the donkey cart with the rest of the Gunsbach boys, he would greet Mausche politely, shake hands, and walk a little way along with him. Later, Schweitzer (who was to marry a Jew) fancied that Mausche's tolerant smile taught him what it means to keep silent under persecution and "to be patient when I should like to rage and storm."

By this time he had left Gunsbach village school and, at the age of nine, entered a secondary school in Münster, where he was taught, if not theology, Bible stories by a pastor named Schäffler, who evidently possessed a remarkable talent for making the tales of the ancient Jews as real as if they had happened only a day ago. As he told the entrancing story of Joseph being recognized by his brothers, Pastor Schäffler would himself weep as he sat at his desk. As he wept, every child sitting in his own form would sob with him.

Yet even still, Albert Schweitzer was often ill at ease. To his annoyance and embarrassment, the other boys could easily make him laugh in class. Pastor Schäffler, instead of being provoked to anger by Schweitzer's insubordination, tried to turn this apparent weakness to good, even religious, effect. Loving the Jewish patriarchs, he dubbed Albert Isaac, which means "the laugher."

The stratagem scarcely worked. Albert Schweitzer's passionate temper (inherited, he supposed, from his mother and through her· from Pastor Schillinger, the saintly but quick-tempered man of God) was not tamed by his intelligent, sensitive teacher. Schweitzer needed to tame himself, extravagantly, even doing violence to his inner self. Yet at this early age Albert was already grappling with his inner problems and displaying an astonishing self-knowledge.

The process had begun remarkably early. As Albert had discovered, he not only hated losing at games, but at the same time could not bear a weak or, in his view, unworthy opponent. When he was nine or ten he found himself so easily defeating his sister Adèle in some game that he struck her in the face. Shocked by his own violence, Schweitzer gradually gave up all games, his overwhelming passion for victory being more than his moral sense could bear. Yet in other fields—in his brilliantly provocative religious thought, in the many moral controversies of his life, in the iron rule he was to exercise in the unique jungle hospital he created—Schweitzer's passionate desire to overwhelm any possible opponent survived.

The secondary school at Münster offered Schweitzer the delightful bonus of being two miles away from Gunsbach. The walk through beautiful countryside from his own village to school and back again entranced him. Suddenly, all this came to an end. At the age of ten, his parents decided that he should now be educated in faraway Mulhouse. Their decision was sensible. His married godfather, Great-uncle Louis, lived there. Louis and his wife, Sophie, offered to feed and lodge the growing boy for nothing. More: A small scholarship was at Albert's disposal as the son of a pastor. The school at Mulhouse obviously was better than the village school at Gunsbach and in some respects was superior to Pastor Schäffler's school at Münster.

This was still the era of the Schweitzer family's near-poverty. Albert's mother, with five children at the parsonage, was making every conceivable economy, cooking not with oil but with inferior (and cheaper) lard, seeing her family spend winter in thin summer clothing. Had it not been for his aunt and uncle's generosity, Albert's education would inevitably have been unequal to his latent genius. "Had it not been for their kindness," he later wrote, "my father, who had nothing beyond his slender stipend on which to bring up his large family, could hardly have afforded to send me to such a school."

At the time none of these reasons appealed to the young Albert Schweitzer. Instead, he wrote, "I felt as if I were being torn away from Nature." Only later did he realize how generous these two relatives had been. At first the strictness of their discipline overwhelmed him. In truth, they were doing their best to understand and cope with a wayward, difficult, moody boy, a boy of inner torments, great talents, and the tendency to dream. His aunt sometimes sensed how much he missed the countryside of Gunsbach. One sunny March day as she was ironing, she caught him looking moodily out of the window at the last melting snows on the mountains. To his astonished delight, she said, "Come along, I'll take you for a bit of a walk." Together they walked over the canal, in which blocks of ice still floated, and up the Rebberg. From then on, Albert Schweitzer warmed more to his Aunt Sophie, perceiving with greater clarity that in spite of her pedagogic strictness she had a heart which understood his longings.

His Uncle Louis, who had once run the Franco-German school in Naples, was at that time director of the elementary school of Mulhouse and therefore a convinced pedagogue. Louis believed in laying down in the minutest conceivable detail everything that should happen in his house. For ten-year-old Albert, this involved enduring a school at home, apart from his real school. He had no free time. He had to practice on the piano after lunch until school proper started again. If he finished his homework early in the evening, then he was back on the piano stool. Happily, the practice increasingly ceased to be a chore and became a joy.

By this time he had developed a passion for reading. Only on Sundays, after the family's regular Sabbath walk, could he freely indulge this passion. Even here, Aunt Sophie interfered in what seemed an abominable fashion. Young Albert by now had developed his life-long skill of gutting a book: skimming through it because he could not bear to put any volume down before he had reached the end; sitting up all night if necessary to finish a hefty tome; and then, if he had relished the work, reading it again two or more times.

Aunt Sophie too was a reader, but of a totally different kind. Style rather than content entranced her. She loved the rhetoric of Victor Hugo and the slyly humorous prose of Alphonse Daudet. But since style was everything to her, Aunt Sophie felt no compulsion to devour a book in its entirety at one sitting. For her, reading each evening for three hours, one before supper, two after, while knitting or crocheting sufficed. Young Albert sat with his book at the same table. He never savored the work slowly but rather devoured it as fast as possible. To his well-meaning aunt he seemed merely to be "sniffing through" it. In consequence, if her nephew reached the end of a volume too fast, she was disturbed; perhaps Albert's education would be affected for the worse. So she alternately chided, scoffed, or attempted to persuade her charge with kindness to follow her own pattern. Only by reading more slowly, she urged, would Albert truly come to appreciate the style of a work.

Albert knew better, but did not dare say so. In his view, his own pattern of reading gauged a book's style perfectly. The more sentences he found it necessary to skip, the more badly written he deemed the book to be. On the other hand, "If it so entranced me that I could not help reading every sentence, I considered that the style must be good." But he kept all this superior insight to himself, fearful of irritating Aunt Sophie by revealing his true views, for in the matter of reading she held him entirely in her power: She alone decided whether he was to be granted a quarter of an hour more or a quarter of an hour less with his beloved books.

In later years Albert Schweitzer would minimize and even try to conceal the perpetual anguish of this period of his youth. "The strict discipline under which I came in the house of my great-uncle and his wife, who had no children of their own, was very good for me," he avowed. "It is with deep gratitude that I constantly think of all the kindness I received from them." Then, suddenly, life in Mulhouse began to improve for the sensitive youth. From his mother, Albert had inherited a passion for following the great public events and politics of the day. Though pious and devoted to Sunday as a day of rest, she was also intensely annoyed on those Christian feasts (Boxing Day, Easter Monday, and Whitsun) when no daily newspaper appeared. From the age of nine her son began to develop similar passions, avidly following what was going on in the affairs of the world. As a result, at Mulhouse, when the table was being laid for supper, he would snatch up the daily papers and pore over them.

This habit produced the occasion of a breakthrough in his relationship with his uncle. Aunt Sophie was convinced that the young Albert wanted to read not politics but simply the stories in the literary supplements to the daily newspapers. So she tried to stop him reading newspapers altogether. One evening she told her husband her reasons. Albert's uncle decided to test his charge, then about age eleven, asking him who ruled in the Balkans, what were their prime ministers called, who had served in the previous three French cabinets, and other such questions. Albert answered every question correctly (though in truth he also loved reading the stories in the literary supplements). From that moment, his uncle saw him in a new light. He not only granted Albert permission to read the newspapers after the boy had finished his homework, as well as when the table was being laid, he also began to treat the eleven-year-old as a grown-up and would discuss the politics of the day with him at mealtimes.

For their part, Schweitzer's aunt and uncle in truth had

much to put up with from their charge. First, Albert was a poor scholar. As he himself admitted, "Although it had been considerable trouble to learn to read and write, at the Gunsbach village school and the secondary school in Münster I had managed fairly well. At the Mulhouse school however I was initially an inadequate pupil." Part of the problem was that the Münster secondary school had not taught him Latin. He had been given some private lessons, but these had not proved enough to prepare him properly for a fifth-form education. Happily, Albert Schweitzer came across one of those schoolmasters who recognize genius hidden in the most unlikely pupils. Dr. Wehmann, as the dreamy Schweitzer perceived, was an exemplary teacher, coming to each lesson extremely well prepared, giving back carefully marked exercise books exactly when the children expected them, and knowing precisely what he wanted to teach and how he would achieve it. "I should have been ashamed to incur his displeasure," Schweitzer wrote, "and he became my model." His Christmas school report had been so bad that his mother spent the whole of the holiday weeping. Three months later his Easter report placed him among the best pupils.

Schweitzer never forgot Dr. Wehmann. He would call upon him as Wehmann's career progressed by way of Mulhouse to Thann, Saargemünd, and finally Strasbourg. One day shortly after the end of World War I Schweitzer returned to seek out the excellent doctor. Wehmann, he discovered, had been so much reduced by poverty and starvation that he had killed himself.

A second problem was that at the age of fourteen the introverted Albert Schweitzer suddenly found his voice. For the next two years the noise the boy set up was intolerable. His passion for discussion annoyed everyone, even his father, who liked conversation. "I emerged from the shell of reserve in which up till now I had hidden myself and became the one who disrupted every amiable conversation," Albert remembered. His aunt scolded him as an insolent child who wanted to argue with adults as if they were his age. Whenever the Schweitzer family went to pay a visit, his father insisted that the teenage boy promise not to spoil the day by "stupid behavior during conversations." Albert comforted himself with the thought that his new pattern of life sprang from the spirit of light- and truth-seeking he had inherited from his grandfather Schillinger.

Still, he was at last beginning to learn. His best subject was history. He loved natural science (though it was badly taught in most of his schools), but languages and mathematics had always been difficult for Albert. Now he began to experience a fascination with mastering subjects for which he possessed no special talent. He felt himself fortunate that his next Greek and Latin master, an apparently dry-as-dust native of Lübeck named Wilhelm Deecke, was not only passionate about ancient philosophy but also an enthusiastic protagonist of the teachings of Arthur Schopenhauer. Among Deecke's friends were the poet Emanuel Geibel and the historian Theodor Mommsen. He himself was an authority on early Greek inscriptions and Etruscan archaeology. He would read Plato to his amazed and delighted students and discuss philosophy with them.

Schweitzer's good fortune was the result of Deecke's ill fortune. His teacher's natural candor had enraged the authorities, who had punished him by reducing Deecke to a lower grade of teacher. Deecke endured the degradation cheerfully, to the astonishment of his more discerning pupils. As Albert Schweitzer later put it, "He was for us a Stoic in modern dress." Just as he was about to be rehabilitated, this gifted teacher died of cancer of the stomach.

Albert Schweitzer also was developing the independent mind that in later years would so astound the learned world. Characteristically, he expressed his new-found independence provocatively. Whenever his teachers asked the class to discuss poetry, young Albert became incensed. "That a poem should be brought nearer to me by being explained I felt to be something hateful and silly," he declared. "The talk about it did nothing but destroy in me the feeling of being possessed by the work of the poet." A poem, he believed throughout his life, does not need to be explained but to be experienced. So in poetry lessons he became an exceedingly inattentive scholar, or rather (as he put it) "a scholar in opposition." Without the benefit of his schoolmas-

ters as guides, he would sit in class exploring the poetry textbook on his own, intoxicating himself with those poems and
extracts he found most attractive. It was as if, he said, he had
"shut the shop-windows so as to keep out the noise in the
streets."

Such enthusiasms delight only the most discerning peda-
gogues. They do not lead to outstanding exam results. Not surprisingly, Albert Schweitzer did not leave his Mulhouse school
with the finest scholastic honors. The final examination took
place on June 18, 1893. At the age of nineteen Albert passed, but,
as he wrote, "I did not cut a brilliant figure."

In the viva, his examiner was the school commissioner from
Strasbourg, a Dr. Albrecht. Examinees were required to wear a
black frock coat and a pair of black trousers. Albert had inherited
an old black frock coat from one of his mother's relatives. He
possessed no black trousers. Since the Schweitzer family was
still poor, Albert refused to have a new pair of trousers made for
the occasion but instead borrowed a pair from his great-uncle.
Uncle was short and stout. Albert was tall and thin. When he
dressed on the morning of the examination the trousers barely
reached his shoes, even though he had lengthened his braces
with string. Between the trousers and his waistcoat yawned an
extensive gap. Behind him they flapped like an oversize sack.

Naturally enough, everyone joined in the merriment save
school commissioner Albrecht, who expressed himself severely
on the irreverent behavior caused by this ungainly pupil. His initial response was to grill Schweitzer unmercifully, especially
about Homer (whose poetry had always left the boy cold). Then
came history, the school commissioner's own special subject. "In
ten minutes," Schweitzer recalled, "he seemed a different person. His indignation melted away." Together, pupil and examiner ardently discussed the differences between the Greek colo-
nists and the Romans. In his final address Dr. Albrecht went out
of his way to mention the pleasure this discussion had given
him. Albert Schweitzer's fairly mediocre diploma was adorned
by Albrecht's special commendation.

Religion and education in Alsace, so powerfully represented

by Albert Schweitzer's parents and ancestors, bequeathed to the growing boy two further priceless legacies: a love of music, especially organ music, and a passion for theology. Albert surmised that his love of the first derived from his Grandfather Schillinger. But his first lessons came from his father. Louis-Théophile Schweitzer began teaching his son at the age of five on the old square piano which the family had inherited from Grandfather Schillinger.

Pastor Johann Jakob Schillinger himself was a superb improvisatore on the organ. He was fascinated by the instrument. The first thing he did on visiting a new town was to seek out the church organs. When the celebrated organ at the Collegiate Church of Lucerne was being built, Pastor Schillinger left his parish and spent days there watching the master organ builders at work.

Albert had inherited this passion. The sound of his parents singing ancient Alsatian songs in two-part harmony so thrilled him that he became weak with ecstasy and had to lean against a wall. He was but nine years old when he first substituted for the organist at his father's Gunsbach church. Soon the gifted child was working out harmonies of his own. "I did not play much from notes," he remembered. "My delight was to improvise, and to reproduce songs and hymn tunes with an accompaniment of my own invention." At school he was surprised to find that the singing teacher simply played tunes with one finger, adding not the slightest accompaniment. Albert openly asked her why she did not play them "properly," with harmony, and he promptly sat down at the harmonium and played a hymn out of his own head, adding a four-part harmony. To her credit, the teacher thenceforth became his friend, regarding him with a new and unusual appreciation, but she continued to pick out a tune herself with one finger. For the first time, it occurred to Albert that he could do something she could not. In his customary fashion he became confused and ashamed at this alarming knowledge. He had made a show before her of an ability that hitherto he had taken to be something he possessed like everyone else, simply as a matter of course.

In Mulhouse, at the age of fifteen, he found a yet greater teacher, Eugen Münch. With a passion for the works of Bach, Münch had just arrived from the Berlin Music High School to take up the post of organist at the Calvinist Church of Saint Stephen. At first he could scarcely bear teaching his curmudgeonly pupil. "Albert Schweitzer is a thorn in my flesh," he would cry. Two problems were coming between them. One was that Albert was still improvising on his aunt's piano (partly because she insisted that he sight-read) instead of properly learning the pieces Münch set him. Second, his innate shyness inhibited him from displaying to Münch all he was emotionally and technically capable of. Instead, all Münch heard was wooden and unfeeling.

The teacher one day reacted with justified anger. Albert had just played a badly practiced sonata by Mozart. The irate Münch opened a copy of Mendelssohn's E-natural "Song without Words," commenting, "You really have no right to be asked to play such beautiful music. You'll now come and spoil this musical composition for me, just as you have spoiled everything else." Eugen Münch ended his tirade with the insult, "If a boy has no feeling, it's certain that I can't give him any."

The technique worked. "Oho!" thought the nettled Schweitzer, "I'll show you whether or not I have any feeling." Throughout the following week he practiced the piece again and again. Although no one had yet taught him fingering, he worked out the best way of playing it, noting it above the score. When his next lesson with Münch took place, Albert Schweitzer patiently sat through the exercises with his fingers and with scales. Then he braced himself and played Medelssohn's E-natural "Song without Words" from the depths of his soul.

At the end Eugen Münch hardly spoke. Placing his hands firmly on Albert's shoulders, he moved the boy from the piano and sat down there himself. Then he played for the boy another Mendelssohn "Song without Words" that Albert had never heard.

A year later Münch allowed his sixteen-year-old pupil to take his place at services in Mulhouse. Not long afterward

Albert was trusted by his distinguished teacher to play the organ accompaniment to Brahms's *Requiem*, sung by the choir of Saint-Etienne, Mulhouse. "Then, for the first time, I knew the joy—which I have so often savored since—of letting the organ send the flood of its own unique tones to mingle with the powerful music of the choir and the orchestra," Albert wrote.

Eugen Münch's legacy to Albert Schweitzer (and thus to humanity) is incalculable. Schweitzer himself acknowledged the debt. His very first publication was devoted to the music of Bach but appeared in the form of a deeply affectionate obituary of Münch. This appreciation of his teacher appeared in print when Schweitzer was a mere twenty-three years old. One of the copies in the Schweitzer archive is annotated in Schweitzer's own hand with the proud inscription, "The first of my writings to be published," and the additional admonition, "Don't take this copy away with you."

Bach's *The Well-tempered Clavier*, says Schweitzer, was from Münch's childhood his teacher's daily bread. (Oddly enough Schweitzer never grew to like the work. As he told his Spanish friend Lluis Millet in 1911, the vibration of the clavier's strings made his own intestines vibrate, resulting in diarrhea.) Writing of Münch's years as organist at Mulhouse, Schweitzer once again displays his own extraordinary notion that organs possess almost human qualities by telling us that the instrument in the Protestant parish church entirely accorded in its tones with Münch's personality. Its powerful sound and its finesse matched the refinements of registration at which he excelled, while certain mechanical defects forced Münch to play with a calmness that produced both tranquillity and majesty.

Schweitzer recalled that Münch's favorite pieces were Bach's Toccata in D Minor and his Passacaglia in C Minor—two works that were to number among his own favorites. And he taught the young Schweitzer a word which repeatedly recurs in his own writings on Bach: "plasticity." Münch also instilled in Schweitzer a lifelong preference for playing the organ in churches rather than in concert halls.

Yet Münch eventually came to perceive that secular music

could approach the heights of religious music. The revelation came for him at the Wagner shrine at Bayreuth. "There he vividly realized how much the masterpieces of tragic music, by virtue of their value and beauty, carry within themselves the character of religion."

This man, who so influenced his pupil, remained curiously distant. Schweitzer recalled that only among his intimate family did he ever loosen up. "At Mulhouse he had many friends but no comrades." Apart from the pupils whom he had known as children, he never used the intimate address *Tu*, always preferring the more formal *Vous*. Schweitzer meditated on the black depressions with which he was sometimes assailed. Maybe, he speculated, Münch had a premonition of his early death. Schweitzer touchingly describes the last time his teacher played the Mulhouse organ, so worn out that he could scarcely finish the service. Convalescing at Niederbronn, Münch visibly weakened, unable even to carry his youngest child in his arms. Constantly asking how was his beloved organ in Mulhouse, he heard a distant regiment signaling the retreat. "It is the signal that prepares me for my end," he murmured. Then he consoled himself with the words, "I shall be an organist in heaven."

Albert Schweitzer's own playing now began to entrance others too. "The most beautiful treasures of all my memories of this time," wrote his niece and goddaughter Suzanne Oswald, known as Suzi, "are those evenings when my uncle played the organ in our church at Gunsbach." Often too she would exult in the music as he played the Münster church organ for a couple of friends—reveling in Bach's Prelude and Fugue in G Minor, which lit up the empty, dark church, and in his interpretations of César Franck and Mendelssohn.

A second legacy of Schweitzer's Gunsbach home was his fascination with the Bible, the Holy Writ of Protestant Christianity. This was a doubly valuable legacy, for it also involved a profound conviction of the reality of the Jesus who, in Protestant dogma, crowns that biblical witness. In consequence, Schweitzer's lifelong questioning of his own religious tradition never threatened the inner core of his faith. This quasi-mystical element in his inheritance is an enigmatic key to his personality. "People say that those who do theology are confronted with hard battles, because of the doubts which arise when they plunge themselves into the deep study and research of Christian doctrine and history," he told a Strasbourg congregation in April 1904. He then added the astonishing claim that he himself had never for a moment suffered such problems. "Such doubts and temptations have never assailed me," he said, "because I have been so certain of His spiritual presence."

In his Strasbourg sermons it is evident that Schweitzer was exploring his own inner conflicts and convictions as well as addressing those of his congregations. On another Sunday in April 1904, for instance, he preached from the pulpit of Saint-Nicolas what he called a message to all doubters. "Let everything else go, so long as you hold on to this one truth: Jesus is a man who demands your help in the work He Himself began. If you respond, His glorious presence will overwhelm you, and you will become rich—far richer than you can possibly imagine." Schweitzer's beliefs about Jesus apparently ceased to be a problem for him the moment he acted on Jesus's impossible commands.

From his earliest years this passion for the Bible, and in particular the New Testament, never involved an uncritical acceptance of every word of Scripture as infallibly true. Albert Schweitzer was a true grandchild of Pastor Schillinger, that son of the Enlightenment. This unflinchingly rationalist inheritance already caused Albert difficulties when the time came for him to be confirmed as a full adult member of the Christian church. He greatly respected the venerable old Pastor Wennagel, who trained him for confirmation, but he never dared ask the kindly pastor all the questions that were stirring in his heart. On one matter they profoundly disagreed, though Albert still kept silent. Pastor Wennagel insisted that submission to the Christian faith required the believer to silence all the demands of reason. By contrast, Albert Schweitzer was convinced that the fundamental principles of Christianity must be revealed as true by reason, and by nothing else. He remained so convinced all his life.

"Reason, I said to myself, is given to us that we may bring every-thing within the range of its action, even the most exalted ideas of religion."

The thought filled him with joy. It did not, however, appeal to Pastor Wennagel. Perceiving this, when he was brought face to face with the pastor for the most intimate and private discussion before his confirmation, Albert merely prevaricated, refusing to let the old pastor look right into his heart and question his true beliefs. The pastor was disturbed. He told Schweitzer's aunt that Albert was one of those indifferent candidates, going forward for confirmation without any real conviction. The reverse was true. "In reality," wrote Schweitzer, "during those weeks I was so moved by the holiness of the time that I felt almost ill." Pastor Wennagel's doubts happily did not detract from the magic of the occasion. On Palm Sunday, when Albert Schweitzer was confirmed, he walked in procession from the vestry of Saint Stephen's Church, Mulhouse, while Eugen Münch played the Psalm "Lift up your heads, O ye gates," in the setting of Handel's *Messiah*. The love of reason did not for Albert Schweitzer involve rejecting passion, for he was passionate about reason.

Louis-Théophile Schweitzer had given his son a New Testament when he reached the age of eight. The gift was at Albert's own request. He read it eagerly but already critically. In his first year at school Albert had questioned his father about the Flood, as recounted in the Old Testament. That summer was a wet one. He asked his father why, since it had rained for nearly forty days and forty nights, the tops of the Gunsbach houses, let alone the peaks of the Vosges Mountains, had not been covered with water, as the biblical story might indicate. Pastor Louis answered his small son, "At the beginning of the world it did not rain just in drops but in bucketfuls." Later, when Albert's schoolmistress told her class the story of the Flood, the pastor's son was astonished that she didn't mention this invented fact and impatiently called out from his seat, "Teacher, you must tell the story correctly."

Possessed of his own New Testament, he became fascinated by Saint Matthew's story of the Magi who brought the infant Jesus gifts of gold, frankincense, and myrrh. "What did the parents of Jesus do with the gold and other valuable gifts they obtained from these men, I asked myself? How could they have been poor after that?" And Schweitzer puzzled over the incomprehensible fact that these so-called Wise Men apparently never troubled themselves again about the child Jesus. When he turned to the opening chapters of Saint Luke's Gospel, he was similarly puzzled. "The absence of any record of the shepherds of Bethlehem," who, it was written, had worshipped the Christ child, "becoming disciples, gave me a severe shock."

Ten years later and thus equipped, after a brief interlude in Paris Albert Schweitzer followed in his father's footsteps and entered the theological faculty of the University of Strasbourg.

CHAPTER 3

◆

Interludes in Paris and a Lifetime of Music

etween the ages of 16 and 18 I found battling within myself
a dispute over whether my calling should be in the field of
music or of theology," Schweitzer confessed. Music drew
him powerfully. "I longed to become organist of a beautiful
church." At the age of sixteen these musical longings had been
powerfully reinforced by his first taste of Wagner. As a Mulhouse schoolboy he had been allowed to go to the theatre at
Bayreuth for the first time. "I heard there Wagner's *Tannhäuser*,"
he recalled. "This music overpowered me to so great an extent
that days passed before I was able to start properly concentrating on my lessons again."

At first glance, Schweitzer's interests might seem remarkably diverse. Philosophy and theology were obviously akin.
Religious compassion was the impulse behind his missionary
hospital and his study of medicine. But the musical talents he
displayed and never neglected seem remote from these other
passions—an excrescence on the rest.

In fact, the boy whose inner self had been torn by emotional
anxiety increasingly became a unified personality, and music

was a fundamental element in it. His Lutheran antecedents helped him here. Lutheranism then as now was a passionately musical facet of the Christian world and Bach its demigod. Among the theology teachers at Strasbourg in Schweitzer's day were Julius Smend, whose father had been an authority on Bach, and Friedrich Spitta, whose brother had written the composer's biography. Schweitzer's writings on Bach (*Bach le musicien-poète*, which appeared in 1905; the considerably expanded German version of 1908; the revised and corrected English version of 1911; and the eight volumes of Bach's organ works that were published by the American firm of Schirmer) were in an important sense a part of his religious vocation and thus an essential element in his complex self.

He said so himself. Discovering that Oskar von Hase, the director of Breitkopf and Härtel, which was to publish his first book on Bach, was a godson of the theologian Eduard Reuss, Schweitzer wrote that if old Reuss had discovered that he was writing a book on music rather than theology, he would have struck Schweitzer with his stick. But, he went on to assert, music was for him as much a spiritual as an intellectual vocation. "In short, to plunge your whole soul in Bach is exactly the same as doing theology." And there is a clear parallel (especially in Volume VI of his edition of Bach) between Schweitzer's comparative analysis of the various editions of Bach's works and the way he and his fellow theologians collated the variations in the first three Gospels and then tried to determine what was authentically historical, what authentically derived from Jesus himself.

But Albert Schweitzer was also the dutiful, if at times rebellious, son of a pastor who had revered the great Protestant preacher Johannes Mathesius. Herein lay the conflict between theology and the appeal of music. "I felt that my part also lay with the preaching of God's word," said Albert Schweitzer, "for from my youth I had understood the text 'Lord I love the situation of your house and the place where your honor dwells'," he told Oskar Pfister. "Always a passionate longing for the church and its solemnities moved me," a longing he later traced back to the intimate Sunday afternoon services conducted by his father in Gunsbach. So Schweitzer chose to read theology and philosophy at Strasbourg; but in the gap between leaving school and beginning his studies at Strasbourg, he indulged his other passionate calling by pursuing a musical interlude in Paris.

In all probability Albert's family was glad to see him go. The organ on which he practiced required his sisters to pump the bellows ceaselessly, and Albert seemed oblivious to the fact that sometimes they wished to do something else. His incessant practicing on the piano also drove those who had to endure the noise almost crazy, for Albert repeatedly played scales and arpeggios while others wanted quiet.

When he reached Paris, he was no country bumpkin fallen among sophisticates. Albert Schweitzer was cared for by relatives of considerable achievement, despite Jean-Paul Sartre's hatred of them. He took lodgings with his Uncle Auguste, a businessman of much acumen. And his Uncle Charles introduced him to intellectual Parisian society.

Charles was a *docteur ès lettres* and a teacher of German at the College Janson de Saylly. He had been one of the founders of the Insitute of Living Languages, a haunt of young German immigrants in Paris, and also was writing what proved to be a successful textbook on the teaching of French. He had married the daughter of a Mâcon solicitor, who bore him four children. One of his daughters married a marine officer, with whom, before his premature death, she conceived their illustrious, malevolent son Jean-Paul Sartre.

On this heady visit, Albert Schweitzer discovered and learned to exploit his long-concealed social graces. He was asked to be best man at a wedding. The groom was a Herr Herrenschmidt. But most extraordinary is that the shy Schweitzer danced the whole night through. Also at this wedding, he met the bridegroom's sister, an unmarried teacher of forty. In spite of the difference in age, the two conceived a powerful attraction for each other. She too was an Alsatian, named Adèle, and soon she was appointed principal of a young ladies' finishing school. Every year before World War I, when Albert Schweitzer took his annual holiday, Adèle Herrenschmidt took it with him, both of them living in an isolated Swiss inn near Interlaken, accompanied by, among others, the young daughter of the groom whose best man Schweitzer had been.

The precise nature of their relationship has proved impossible to decipher. Adèle Herrenschmidt died in 1920, and the reticent Schweitzer wrote in his memoirs the evasive, laconic remark, "When I was in Paris I saw much of Mlle. Adèle Herrenschmidt, a woman from Alsace whose profession was teaching." He added nothing more. Rightly or wrongly, Paris traditionally was seen as the home of romantically flirtatious women. Here too, on his next visit, Albert Schweitzer met another vivacious, unmarried, and talented Alsatian woman, Marie Jaëll-Trautmann, a former disciple of Franz Liszt. She had been a composer herself and had abandoned the profession to promote her own theories of piano playing. From her Schweitzer learned a theory of fingering and touch which involved a technique of mental and physical relaxation.

Marie Jaëll-Trautmann's students were shown how to free their muscles from any tension, so that the flow between psyche and fingers would be instinctive and uninterrupted. She believed that the finger itself would then recognize which sound it wished to produce from the keyboard. Sensitivity was her own keynote. She would bring in physiologists to help her and her pupils in this aim. And, if his own boast is to be believed, she made Schweitzer's fingers sensitive. "Increasingly I mastered my fingers," he wrote, "with a consequent significant improvement in the way I played the organ."

Lubricious and maliciously discourteous comments have been made about such friendships by Schweitzer's detractors. The truth is that the young man was at last unbending, learning that deep friendship, and in his case, friendship with more mature women, could be combined with his commitment to his own vocation. This was a vital lesson he never forgot. Nonetheless, Schweitzer amusingly displayed a newly found and charming cunning when dealing with attractively temperamental women, a gift that was to stand him in good stead for the rest of his life. In Paris he coolly kept secret from his friend Marie Jaëll-Trautmann another part of his life. Had she learned of it, he felt certain the fact would have upset her. He also was taking piano lessons from one of her rivals, J. Philipp, soon to become a teacher at the Paris Conservatoire. "The instruction I gained from Philipp, moving as it did along the more traditional paths of piano-teaching, was also extraordinarily valuable," he publicly confessed some years after Marie's death in 1925, "protecting me from what was one-sided in the Jaëll method." At the time, however, since neither of his piano tutors could stand the other, neither learned that Albert was two-timing them. "What a trouble it cost me to play à la Jaëll with Marie Jaëll in the morning and à la Philipp with Philipp in the afternoon!" the deceiver later admitted.

Though regarding Marie's techniques as one-sided, Albert Schweitzer nonetheless paid her a generous tribute: "I owe it to her that by well-directed practice taking but little time, I became more and more completely the master of my fingers, greatly to the benefit of my organ-playing." When the German publishers Breitkopf and Härtel brought out an edition of Marie's French textbook, Albert was her anonymous translator.

She also strengthened in him what remained for Albert Schweitzer the centrally important belief that music has deep spiritual dimensions: "Beginning with the physiology of the piano touch, she wanted to ascend to a theory about the nature of art in general. Thus around her entirely correct and forceful observations on the nature of artistic technique she wrapped considerations about the relations between nature and art, considerations that were sometimes odd and unconvincing but were also often thoughtful and profound."

Partly under Marie Jaëll-Trautmann's influence, partly from what he had unconsciously imbibed from his own family, it was becoming increasingly clear to Schweitzer that for a nineteenth-century German Lutheran, music was by no means at odds with theology but instead was a virtually essential complement to it. Karl Budde, who would be Schweitzer's Old Testament professor at Strasbourg and soon a firm friend, was another for whom music offered both an entry into heaven and an escape from the potentially overwhelming torments of a speculative academic life. In this sphere his influence on Albert Schweitzer has never been properly explored. But, as Budde's obituarist recorded, "He played the piano masterfully, and to the end he sang in the choir." Masterfully is a key word, for Budde and for Schweitzer. Even when relaxing and escaping from the problems of their daily lives, these German intellectuals still emotionally and intellectually dominated their escape routes—Budde first, as Albert Schweitzer was himself to do later.

They took on one superhuman task and then proceeded to achieve more. Not content with playing the piano superbly, Karl Budde published acclaimed collections of Old Dutch folksongs and medieval German Christmas carols. He translated a famous Dutch song that became an equally celebrated German lied, "Wir treten zum Beten." As his obituarist trenchantly observed, "All his work was an expression of his personality. He had a strong character and a powerful will," adding, "He was full of enthusiasm and vital energy, an inspiring teacher and a great lecturer, keen in debate, with striking argumentative power; fearless, outspoken, a severe critic of faulty and misleading work, but generous in praise of true and good workmanship." The obituarist could have been describing Budde's pupil, Albert Schweitzer himself, more than fifty years before Schweitzer's death.

In Paris too Schweitzer flung himself enthusiastically into the voluntary choir that one of his friends and fellow Alsatians, Gustàve Bret (a pupil of César Franck) founded in 1905 to sing the passions and cantatas of Bach. Alsatians had a tradition of founding such choirs and of despairingly seeing them fold up. Schweitzer was an enthusiastic member and the society's organist until he left for Lambaréné in 1913. As organist of the latest venture in this field, Schweitzer found the task so taxing that he was moved to write what he called "a social-musical study" for the Berlin journal *Die Musik* on the problems he encountered. For one thing, he pointed out, "A young girl from good, bourgeois and genuine Parisian circles cannot join a choir, since she cannot go out without a chaperone." Until some American-style "emancipation" came about, choirs in Paris would lack sufficient sopranos. In addition, the Parisian tramcar system was so inadequate that choir members—again, especially women—if they came to rehearsals at all were obliged to come by carriage.

Other tediously ingrained habits included the singers' insistence on rehearsing seated, the fact that both men and women kept their hats on while singing, and the frequent intermittent pauses they insisted on. Whereas every German regarded singing in a choir as an essential part of his or her education, the French had never perceived this as a virtue. Never would any choir member agree to prolonging a rehearsal. Finally, the innate individualism of the French made it almost impossible for them to submit to the discipline involved in belonging to a choir. As Schweitzer put it, "The modern Frenchman has an innate anxiety about anything called discipline, regarding it as nothing less than the submission which is unworthy of a free spirit."

Schweitzer had gone to Paris not primarily to meet mature women pianists, to help run a Bach choir, or to join the intellectual and financial circles inhabited by his relatives. Again, the multiple aspects of his personality were to the fore. His aim was in part to study the religious philosophy of Kant at the Sorbonne and also to practice the organ under one of the most distinguished performers and teachers of the age, Charles-Marie Widor. The two men instantly delighted in each other, and their subsequent collaboration immeasurably enhanced the musical scholarship of the twentieth century.

The French organist, teacher of music, and composer Charles-Marie-Jean-Albert Widor had been born in Lyon on February 12, 1844. Hungarian blood ran through his veins, derived from his organ-building grandfather and his organ-building father. Widor learned to play the organ on his father's knee. So brilliantly did he perform that by the age of eleven he was organist at the Lyon Lycée. Aristide Cavaillé-Coll, one of the most remarkable of nineteenth-century French organ builders, recommended that the young Widor should be sent to Brussels, to learn composition with a genius named Fétis and to enhance his skills as an organist under J. N. Lemmens. This connection with Lemmens gave Widor an insight into the then absurdly neglected works of Johann Sebastian Bach, so that when Schweitzer arrived in Paris, fired with a love of Bach from his Mulhouse teacher Eugen Münch, there was already an avant-garde affinity between them. Lemmens, whose own teachers stretched back in an unbroken line to Bach himself, interpreted Bach in a Germanic fashion which his French pupil made his own. Again Schweitzer, half-German, half-French, would meet in Paris a teacher who understood his own diverse, complex, and rich musical background.

After his studies in Brussels, Widor's subsequent progress was dazzlingly swift. From 1860 to 1870 he was organist at the Church of Saint-François, Lyons, consolidating his reputation elsewhere as a concert organist. Then in 1870 he succeeded Louis Lefebure-Wély as organist at the Church of Saint-Sulpice, Paris. During the Franco-Prussian War, which began in that year, Widor helped to defend Paris, but he rode back from the fortifications each Sunday morning to play at Saint-Sulpice. As he later told his pupil Marcel Dupré, "I do not recommend you ever to attempt to play on the pedals while you are wearing spurs." The appointment at Saint-Sulpice was provisional, lasting initially only for one year, and Widor did not intend to lose the position. It was speedily confirmed, and there Charles-Marie Widor stayed for the next sixty-four years.

Next, while retaining his post as organist at Saint-Sulpice (where his patron, the great Aristide Cavaillé-Coll, had recently rebuilt the organ), Charles-Marie Widor succeeded César Franck as teacher of the organ at the Paris Conservatoire. He now had the pick of the organ students of western Europe. Into his presence came the still bulky but recently emancipated Albert Schweitzer. Alas, en route to his first interview with the great man, Albert was held up by a Parisian traffic jam. When he finally arrived, late for his appointment, the dapper Widor with his cavalry mustache was waiting with impatience. He asked Schweitzer what he wished to play. Unerringly, Albert answered, "Naturally, Bach." No answer could have been better. Widor, the Bach lover, listened to the performance of Eugen Münch's sullen pupil. The teacher broke a lifelong rule of caution and instantly accepted his would-be pupil.

The rapport between master and pupil was remarkable. Each complemented the other's genius. Both smoked; both loved to flatter pretty women; and both shared a quasi-mystical devotion to their chosen musical instrument. Schweitzer remembered his tutor telling him one afternoon, as they sat together on the organ bench of Notre-Dame-de-Paris, that to play the organ "is the manifestation of a will filled with a vision of eternity." The whole purpose of teaching the organ, said Widor that afternoon, is "to educate a person to this pure manifestation of the higher will."

What Widor gained from Schweitzer was an understanding of the symbolism of Bach's compositions, a symbolism based essentially on an understanding of the texts of the chorales and cantatas which the younger man, who was, after all, a Lutheran theologian, was able to elucidate. In 1899 Widor considered Bach's chorales "cloudy," whereas he could perceive the movement of his preludes and fugues as logical and clear. When he told his pupil this, Schweitzer responded that the chorales could be understood only through their texts. At the same time, Schweitzer insisted that Bach was essentially a mystic rather than a coldly calculating theologian. For this reason, he declared, in Bach's works the musical painting at times enormously intensifies the meaning of the words which it sets, transforming this meaning into something far more emotionally intense.

If we exempt the hints in Schweitzer's memoir of his tutor Eugen Münch, his earliest published views on Bach appear in a piece he wrote for the *Revue Germanique* in 1905. "Bach was a poet, and this poet was at the same time a painter," it begins. Then for six pages Schweitzer entirely neglects the ostensible subject of his article in order to point out that Friedrich Schiller was also a musician and a poet; that Goethe long hesitated between the vocations of poet and painter; that Gottfried Keller, celebrated for his *Romeo and Juliet*, began his career as a painter; that Nietzsche submitted compositions to Wagner. A couple more pages manage to speak of Michelangelo and Veronese.

Then the flaccid article bursts into life as Schweitzer begins to analyze Bach's works. In Cantata no. 176 (*"Es ist ein trotzig, und verzagt Ding"*), he asserts, Bach, though supposedly dedicated to writing a piece of music expressing contrition, had seized on the word *trotzig* ("arrogant") and made it the central point of the work. When Schweitzer considers Cantata no. 88 (*"Siehe, ich will viel Fischer aussenden"*), the analysis employs the same technique, this time fixing on the word for "fisher" and depicting Bach's music as evoking the waves of a lake.

The assuredness with which Schweitzer characterizes the essence of each work is riveting. Of Cantata no. 70 (*"Wachet! betet!"*), in the sound of the the the trumpet, says Schweitzer, we hear the call to the Last Judgment. Bach's *Orgel-büchlein* he sees as blending the fear of death with a joyful welcome to eternal life. The *St. Matthew Passion*, for Schweitzer, admirably seeks contrasts, oppositions, and graduations in its music. And, from the evidence of this remarkable article, Schweitzer himself clearly conceived the tones of the organ in colors. He tells us that in Cantata no. 77 (*"Du sollt Gott, deinen Herren, lieben"*), you can hear the bass pipes of the organ sounding white, while the trumpets perform in black.

"Bach's musical language," he wrote, "is the most developed and the most precise that exists." Only in his later works does he step across the boundaries of music, Schweitzer believed. The chorales of 1736 on the Baptism and the Last Supper do so, and Schweitzer confesses that he could scarcely bear to listen to Cantata no. 100 (*"Ich glauben, lieber Herr, hilf meinem Unglauben"*). But he ends with a magnificent tribute to his hero. Just as Goethe, longing in his *Faust* to create the supreme drama, wrote a work that is virtually unplayable in the theatre, so in the later works of Bach the intensity of his thought fought against the musical beauty of his compositions. "Yet," Schweitzer concludes, "his errors were those which only a genius was capable of committing."

This intenseness and this mysticism obviously struck a chord in Schweitzer's own consciousness. As he set off for French Equatorial Africa for the first time in 1913, in Schweitzer's baggage were forty-six volumes of Bach's works. Even when he was

interned in a French concentration camp and in the hospital at
Saint-Rémy-de-Provence, Schweitzer refused to let adverse circumstances interrupt his love for Bach and his skill in performing Bach's works. Glum as his conditions were in those months,
each day he would mentally go over Bach's works before tap-
ping them out on the side of a table.

As with his religious writings, so too his writings on Bach
overthrew many of the preconceptions of his time. When
Schweitzer first began to study the Leipzig composer, Bach was
considered the ideal of rationalism in music, as opposed to the
irrational romanticism of Wagner. But Schweitzer's first awe-
inspiring encounter with music had been at the performance in
Mulhouse of *Tannhäuser*. His Wagnerian enthusiasm restored
poetic romanticism to Bach.

Not surprisingly, in view of this passionate love of Bach,
Schweitzer's last publication, as his first, was devoted to music.
At the age of eighty the old man decided that he had insufficiently enlightened his readers on the subject of the correct execution of Bach's ornamentation and pulled all his energies
together to write an appendix on this theme for the sixth volume
of his edition of Bach's organ works. Finally, in 1967 the last two
volumes of his edition of the works of Bach, coedited by the
Alsatian organist Edouard Nies-Berger, appeared posthumously,
the manuscripts having arrived at the office of the New York
publisher a few days before Schweitzer's death.

His first major attempt to come to terms in print with Bach
had appeared in 1905. In his autobiography Schweitzer declared
that his intention in writing *Bach le musicien-poète* had not been to
produce new historical facts about his subject but to speak of his
music "as a musician addressing fellow-musicians." He set out,
he said, to explore the essential nature of Bach's works and to
determine how to play them. The book met with such an enthusiastic response that German translation was instantly called for.
Schweitzer responded with a version of the book nearly twice as
long as the French original.

Far more magisterial was the eight-volume edition of Bach's
complete organ works, on which he and Widor now collaborated.

Before setting off for Lambaréné in 1913, Schweitzer had the satisfaction of seeing through the press the first five volumes. Not long after his arrival in French Equatorial Africa, the three final volumes were completed, though (because of two world wars, the death of Widor, and financial constraints) these were not published for nearly half a century, with Schweitzer continuing to revise them intermittently until his death. Underlying the edition was the conviction that Bach was neither romantic nor antiromantic, neither a writer of "pure" classical music nor the emotional composer typically interpreted by nineteenth-century performers. Instead, Bach purveyed "the purest religious feeling."

"A poet and painter in sound," Schweitzer wrote, "Bach strives to reproduce in the language of music everything that lies in the text, both emotional and pictorial, with the utmost possible clarity and vitality." For Schweitzer at times it seemed Bach almost was writing program music. "Should the text speak of drifting mists, of boisterous winds, of rushing rivers, of the ebb and flow of waves, of leaves falling from a tree, of bells tolling for the dying, of the confident faith that walks with firm footsteps, of the weak faith which insecurely falters, of the proud who will be humbled, of the humble who will be exalted, of Satan arising in rebellion, of angels on the clouds of heaven, then one sees and hears all of this in his music." Bach's music, he said, was like Gothic architecture transformed into sound. Schweitzer went so far as to attempt to identify precisely what various musical motifs symbolized for Bach, whether joy, anxiety, horror, peace, grief, celebration, death, or resurrection.

Pictures dominate these analyses of Bach's chorales. So, commenting on *"Christum wir sollen loben schon"* at the point where the alto sings the chorale Schweitzer writes, "It seems as if the shepherds and the people have quitted the stable, leaving Mary to rock her baby to sleep by singing a gentle lullaby." *"Christus, der uns selig macht"* is for Schweitzer an almost pictorial depiction of Jesus's arrest and trial, a painting from which "the sinister, complete horror of the text pours out." Similarly *"Da Jesus an dem Kreuze stund"* is a tone picture of the exhausted Savior uttering the seven last words from the cross. Here

Schweitzer is at his most daring, declaring that "the syncopated figuration of the bass describes the bending and raising of the martyred body, a movement also depicted by the inner voices."

Schweitzer's Bach books display the impressive self-confidence of a man raised in the aura of church music and convinced of his own insight into the mind of his musical hero. Not for nothing had he participated in an excavation of Bach's grave and carefully noted the dimensions of the skull of the genius. Confidently Schweitzer declares about *"Christ lag in Todesbanden"* that "the heavily descending movement of the six-teenth-note figuration symbolizes those chains of death which hold Jesus captive." In *"Mit Fried' und Freud' ich fahr' dahin"* he notes that "Bach's typical motif of joy freely triumphs." In *"O Lamm Gottes, unschuldig,"* Schweitzer avers that Bach first por-trays mankind at the foot of the cross and then brings a flash of light to the scene as a host of angels appears above the crucified Savior. As for the first section of *"Jesus Christus, unser Heiland,"* the harsh harmonies suggest that the voices are "whispering to each other the secret of mankind's huge guilt," while the second section of the organ prelude "evokes the picture of mankind scourged by the angry rod of God." Few dared ask how Schweitzer knew these things for certain.

For his writings on Bach Schweitzer sought the help of other experts besides Widor and Edouard Nies-Berger. Two of them were practitioners, so to speak: Berlin lieder singer Georg Walter and founder of the Berlin philharmonic choir Siegfried Ochs. Two were scholars: Théodore Gérold, an expert in lyrical singing, and Gustav Jacobsthal, professor of music at Strasbourg. But Schweitzer remained his own man. Although he knew that none of Bach's organs boasted a swell pedal, he encouraged oth-ers to use one in playing Bach, convinced that Bach himself would have agreed with him. Sometimes, he wrote, a gradual and even crescendo or decrescendo was "called for" in Bach's works, and then—but only then—should the swell be used. Even so, too little of the swell pedal is better than too much: "Better leave the swell pedal severely alone than use it with bad judgment, making the organ sound like an accordion."

In setting out to make both his book on the musician-poet and his edition of Bach's organ works in part practical handbooks for organists, Schweitzer had thus written a book that paralleled his own tireless organ recitals in Germany, France, Italy, Holland, Czechoslovakia, England, Spain, Sweden, Denmark, and Switzerland. The list of venues could have been longer. Invited to play in Russia in late 1915, Schweitzer was prevented by World War I. Invited to perform in the United States in 1936, he pleaded that the demands of his philosophical writings forced him to decline. In Paris too he had become a friend of the Spaniard Lluis Millet, who was later to invite Schweitzer to participate in the concerts he directed in Barcelona. Here he appeared before the king of Spain. After the concert, his majesty asked Schweitzer if playing the organ was difficult. "Almost as difficult as ruling Spain," was Schweitzer's reply.

Bach was not his only standby during these performances. Schweitzer often included in his concerts works by Widor, César Franck, and Felix Mendelssohn. His favorite Widor pieces were the slow movements of his Sixth Organ Symphony. With César Franck Schweitzer usually performed either his "Prayer" for the organ or one of the three chorales written in the last year of the composer's life. As for Mendelssohn, Schweitzer generally played his Fourth or his Sixth Organ Sonata.

One necessary aim of these concerts, which sometimes took him, in the space of a couple of days, from one organ to the next, was to raise money for his missionary hospital. But he also saw himself as a servant of the demigod. When an English listener on his tour of 1934 asked for the autograph of the "celebrated musician," Schweitzer replied, "I am not a 'celebrated musician' but a humble servant of Johann Sebastian Bach."

Twice in the 1930s, and again in 1951 and 1952, he made recordings of the works of Bach. The first, made in a London concert hall for the label His Master's Voice, produced a sound far too harsh for Schweitzer's ear. Then in 1935 he discovered what remained his favorite London organ, that of the Church of All Hallows in the Tower. The Bach Organ Music Society of London was ready to cooperate in promoting these recordings. Circumstances eventually proved this too difficult to arrange, and Schweitzer, along with the whole of Columbia's apparatus and the staff involved, transferred to Strasbourg, where he recorded from the organ of the Church of Sainte-Aurélie. This was an instrument built by Andreas Silbermann in 1718 and restored by Schweitzer's own collaborator, Frédéric Härpfer, under Schweitzer's own instructions.

Again and again Schweitzer recorded and rerecorded until his own exacting standards were finally satisfied. Yet, in what is a delightful paradox, he sometimes used not his own editions of Bach's organ works but that of Peters; and eagle-eared listeners have spotted that in performance he by no means always obeyed the instructions of his own texts.

This organ, considerably enlarged by Schweitzer and Härpfer in 1937, was the same instrument on which he was to record for Columbia Masterworks in the summer of 1952, when Schweitzer was in his midseventies. The previous year he had recorded for the same company a concert on his own beloved organ in Gunsbach church. When his son-in-law tried to dissuade him from this on the grounds that the accoustics of the church muffled the sound, Schweitzer predictably brushed the objection aside.

Schweitzer's recordings are remarkably similar in tempi and tone, suggesting that he had not much changed any of his stances between the 1930s and the 1950s. It is a measure of his stature that not only did these recordings have a profound influence on other musicians and the general public, but also that so much energy has been spent in analyzing them, especially in seeking for musical inconsistencies between them and his writings on Bach. Thus of "An Wasserflüssen Babylon" it has been solemnly noted that Schweitzer's execution of the trills is far from consistent. He begins some on the upper note, but most are incorrectly treated as inverted mordents before the beat. Perhaps it is not so much a criticism of Schweitzer as a measure of the remarkable awe in which he was held that one scholar has even discovered that in recording "Liebster Jesu, wir sind hier" in his later performance, Schweitzer's right hand plays an A instead of the written C in the repeat of the last note of the first measure, as well as an E instead of a G in measure 9, beat 3. The scholar charitably adds that these must be slips of the finger.

Not everyone, then, succumbed entirely to Schweitzer's interpretations of Bach. An admiring article in *The Times* of February 12, 1954, declared that Schweitzer's views on organ-building would be invaluable as the debate gathered momentum on the shape of the new organ to be built in London for the Royal Festival Hall. The critic went on to laud the clarity and definition of Schweitzer's own phrasing. But the article then observed that few English organists would approve of the way Schweitzer enunciated the subject of a fugue on what sounded like a great organ reed, adding that, in his performances, "He takes both toccatas and fugues at a deliberate pace—too slowly, English organists would say."

The Times's music critic failed to note that this apparent slow motion was based on Schweitzer's mature experience. "The more we play Bach's organ works, the slower we take the tempi," he wrote. "Every organist has this experience. The lines must stand out in calm plasticity. There must also be time to bring out their dovetailing and juxtaposition." Undue speed resulted in obscurity and confusion, so that the many organists who imagined that they played Bach "interestingly" by taking him fast had not properly mastered the art of playing. "The better anyone plays Bach, the more slowly he can take the music. The worse he plays him, the faster he must take it."

Schweitzer adduced a convincing technical reason for this stance. "Bach's *adagio, grave* and *lento* are not so slow as ours, nor is his *presto* so fast," he reminded his readers. "Because of this we are easily betrayed into making his slow movements too long drawn-out and of hurrying his fast ones." As he told his pupil Lucie C. Lawson, "Music is not a race, it is a language. One must enunciate clearly and have dignity."

Yet Schweitzer's audacity in interpreting Bach could be breathtakingly cavalier, for he became increasingly convinced that he could look into the mind of the composer he most revered. To avoid the reproach that in playing Bach he omitted some of his master's ornaments, Schweitzer replied that several of the works, according to modern taste, were overladen with them. As he pointed out, "Such pieces are mostly youthful compositions, whereas others are pieces written for the pedal-cembalo." Schweitzer concluded that, "The omission of these ornaments can hardly be regarded as a crime."

In spite of the passion with which he approached these questions, the organ (and at Lambaréné his specially built pedal piano) was also for Schweitzer a release from the turmoil of everyday life. Deeply aware of what he called the "dark of Advent," he discovered that for him *"Nun komm der Heiden Heiland* made the heavenly stars shine out in promise." In 1949, arriving for the first time in the United States, he found the rarefied atmosphere of Aspen, Colorado, a trial to his advancing years. Exhausted by the long voyage, Schweitzer begged access not to a bed or a sofa but to an organ. After an hour he was entirely recovered. Bach, as he had replied to a questionnaire sent out in 1905 by the magazine *Die Musik,* represented for him first and foremost "consolation." Bach represented, he continued, the idea that no one needed the support of mere humans to live an authentic life in this precarious world. Bach combined in his music both a joy in living and a serenity in the face of death. In the primeval forest Schweitzer claimed to have discovered a parallel to that serenity. "When I have lived another couple of years in Africa, I shall feel myself the complete organist," he once said. "I shall have found the peace and quiet which Bach demands."

Organ-building was his second musical passion, and once again he proved a brilliant innovator. On the way back to Alsace from Bayreuth as early as 1896, he had become disillusioned with the current state of organ-building, having called to hear a new organ in the Liederhalle at Stuttgart and been appalled at what he discovered. The experience, he avowed, was akin to Paul's conversion on the Damascus road. His consequent study comparing organ-building in France and Germany appeared in *Die Musik* in 1906. Schweitzer urgently drew attention to the inadequacies of nineteenth-century organs for performing the works of Bach and his contemporaries. His skills were recognized three years later, when the Congress of the International Society of Music held at Vienna set up a section devoted to organ-building and made Schweitzer and his friend Xavier Mathias (of the Catholic Theology Faculty at Strasbourg) joint presidents.

Yet Schweitzer's opinion was far from what he dubbed the archaic notion that Bach's works should be played on the high baroque organs built by the composer's contemporary, Arp Schnitger, or even on the mature organs of the eighteenth-century Silbermann family. "My ideal was a synthesis of the old and the modern organ, retaining from the old the Rückpositif and enriching it with the expressive clavier, keeping to old type of windchest which avoided too high pressures, and above all envisaging an organ in which the main consideration was the beauty and richness of its tone." He deplored the tendency to play Bach on the so-called baroque organs, which were based on those which predated the composer himself. He particularly deplored those who attributed this fashion for baroque organs to his own influence.

For this reason, any organist who attempted to maintain the traditions of Schweitzer himself, and of his master Widor, reaped his thanks. In Saint-Sulpice he once said to Widor's pupil and successor, Marcel Dupré, that the two of them were among the sole surviving representatives of the age when Widor was opening up a new and glorious path for the organ. Then Schweitzer unexpectedly said, "I am going to ask you a favor. I should like you to address me as *tu*." Stupefied, Dupré stammered, "With delight I would have you address me in this way. But from me to you—I could never." But Schweitzer insisted on it.

His birthplace, where France embraced Germany, allowed him to temper the great organs of the Silbermann family with insights gained from the nineteenth-century French organ builder Aristide Cavaillé-Coll. Schweitzer relished an anecdote told him by one of Cavaillé-Coll's assistants: "When one of us worked on something for three weeks and it did not entirely please him, he had the man start again at the beginning; and if the work still failed to please him, the man started again." If most of us did that, the assistant added, we should not stay in business for three months. But Cavaillé-Coll was willing to make enormous sacrifices for his work. Another anecdote to which Schweitzer warmed recounted that Cavaillé-Coll spent 108,000 francs on an organ for Saint-Ouen when the contract specified only 90,000. "I am not sorry I lost money," he declared. "I wanted to create something beautiful." As for Cavaillé-Coll's organ in Saint-Sulpice, Schweitzer wrote that until the day that Paris, like Babel, becomes a heap of rubble, "Those who respond to the magical beauty of his organs will leave Notre-Dame and Saint-Sulpice profoundly meditating on the man who dared in spite of his times to remain a pure artist."

German organs in his day, Schweitzer insisted, were heavy of touch and traction. Insufficiently expressive, they needed more keyboards and much lighter and more diverse voices. Schweitzer's organs embodied the skills of Parisians with the genius of organ builders from Hamburg, Vienna, and Berlin.

Schweitzer believed that only around 1850 was the technique of organ-building sufficiently advanced to realize the ambitions of the Silbermanns themselves. He particularly admired the majestic organ which Aristide Cavaillé-Coll had finished in Paris for the church of Saint-Sulpice in 1862. This was indeed a superb instrument, but to declare that it was ideal for performing the organ works of Bach was a somewhat arbitrary judgment.

In condemning more recent organs, he also discarded their newly invented electrical mechanisms. In part, he simply argued that the techniques of making electrical mechanisms were insufficiently well developed; but it became clear that he disliked them in principle when a revised edition of his book on organ-building appeared in 1927 and still favored mechanical actions. He also wanted softer-toned reeds and, on the great organ, a broad, eight-foot salicional as well as an eight-foot bourdon and an eight-foot flute. The performance of Bach was throughout his overriding guideline, hence his insistence on the French fashion of operating ventils with the feet (since the organist's hands were rarely free while playing the works of the master). He also preferred the French organ's concave pedal boards to the flat ones usually built for German instruments. Soon, new organs were being built in Germany and France according to Schweitzer's principles. He was proud enough to dub the 1909 organ of the Palais de Fêtes, the largest concert hall of Strasbourg, "my" organ.

In his own lifetime Schweitzer was attacked because the baroque organ was not to his taste. But what he achieved in the organs he designed was a union between French expressiveness and German sonority which came to be seen as neoclassical masterpieces. Critics might also point out that Schweitzer never properly distinguished between the organ as used for liturgical purposes and the organ displaying its powers in public concerts. In truth, he was well aware of the differences between concert halls and churches, immensely preferring the latter. He loved to play in the lofty Dutch churches in particular; and—following his first teacher, Eugen Münch—he insisted that what he called "the material presence of stone" was essential if a suitable richness of tone was to replace the harshness of a concert hall. Only if this fullness of tone was "too exhausting" and swamped the voices of a Bach fugue were an organ and its church inadequate. Inevitably, too, he himself failed to live up to some of his own principles, especially the one which insists that any concert performance of a choral prelude should be accompanied by the singing of its corresponding hymn.

Especially dear to him was the organ of Gunsbach, on which he had first learned to play. Damaged in World War I and rebuilt at Schweitzer's own expense in 1932 by the Lorraine firm of Härpfer, the organ was damaged a second time in World War II. Schweitzer determined to raise enough money for a complete rebuilding. He hired the firm of Alfred Kern to reconstruct the organ according to his own specifications, a work completed in 1961. As he wrote, "Thus my last wish in this life is to see that organ solidly rebuilt, to last for ever as a fine mechanically operated instrument. In this way it has been possible for me to construct, in the village which has occupied my thoughts for many long years, the ideal organ: two manuals, pedals, twenty-seven voices in all with which one can play Bach as well as Widor, Franck and Reger."

What was supposed to be Schweitzer's last public concert took place in 1954, when he was eighty. The venue was the Church of Saint-Thomas, Strasbourg; the occasion was the anniversary of the death of Bach; the instrument had been created by Johann Andreas Silbermann, a three-manual organ with forty stops built in the mid–eighteenth century. This was an instrument which he himself had saved from insensitive "restoration" many years previously.

The church was packed, with many people standing. Schweitzer played the Prelude and Fugue in E Minor, the Canzona in D Minor, and the Prelude and Fugue in G major. A choir sang the chorale corresponding to each prelude, for here Schweitzer was able to indulge his passionate insistence that an ideal Bach concert involved an organist playing the preludes and a choir singing the relevant chorale. (Schweitzer did manage to carry this principle to Lambaréné, and frequently his guests and fellow workers would be coerced into forming a scratch choir, which would sing while he played his ancient piano.)

Then he stepped down from the console and announced that he would play the same concert the following day, for the benefit of those who had been obliged to stand during the first performance.

CHAPTER 4

◆

The Young Scholar

Apart from Schweitzer's own genius, the explanation for the cataclysmic effect on the Christian world of his religious writings must partly lie in the inspired teaching of the brilliant theologians whom he encountered at the University of Strasbourg. Most of them were Germans. They soon became Schweitzer's personal friends. The Alsatian Schweitzer came to consider the breathtaking, even arrogant intellectual daring of such men and the stupendous achievements of their discipline as unequaled in the contemporary intellectual world:

> "When, at some future day, our period of civilisation shall lie, closed and completed, before the eyes of later generations, German theology will stand out as a great, a unique phenomenon in the mental and spiritual life of our time," he asserted, adding: "nowhere save in the German temperament can there be found in the same perfection the living complex of conditions and factors of philosophic thought, critical acumen, historical insight, and religious feeling—without which no deep theology is possible."

The central problems, brilliantly tackled if not completely solved by these German theologians, concerned the person of Jesus: Who was he? What was he really like? What was the core of his teaching? Did he or did he not found a church? Did he wrongly predict the imminent end of the world? Did he institute those sacraments, such as Holy Communion and Baptism, which by these theologians' time many considered to be essential elements in the Christian life?

Related to these was the suspicion that the early church had, if not falsified the historical truth about its founder, at least subtly (or sometimes crudely) modified it. For the earliest Christians, the crucified Jesus had rapidly come to be seen as the divine standard of morality, the deliverer of salvation (in this world as well as the next), and the provider of unique insight into the secrets of the universe. Could any human being have been such a person? Had those who wrote about him consciously or unconsciously adapted Jesus's original teaching and the facts of his life to fit their own needs and those of of their own generation? Had they recreated the real Jesus to answer their specific desires and problems?

The key texts about Jesus's life and teachings were the Gospels of Matthew, Mark, Luke, and John. By Schweitzer's time every major Protestant theologian in Germany accepted that these four major documents about Jesus, texts which the church regarded as authentic, were seriously flawed when viewed as historical sources. All four documents, they assumed, had been written at least forty years after the events they purported to describe. Some had been written perhaps more than a hundred years later. Church tradition, probably erroneously, identified their authors, the four evangelists, as men who had known Jesus in his lifetime. All too often these evangelists contradicted each other. Sometimes they even contradicted themselves! They had clearly embellished stories about Jesus. When they described Jesus as teaching by parables, they put into his mouth quite different explanations of the same parable. And to give one disturbing example, all four disagreed about the very last words he spoke when he died on the cross.

Even more startling to men and women convinced that historical truth demanded an utterly rigorous search to discover what actually had happened, these four Gospel writers seemed to find it quite easy to tamper blithely with historical facts about

Jesus. It seemed that they had no qualms about supposing themselves inspired enough to rewrite the record of what had really taken place in the three short years when Jesus taught, suffered, and died.

As for the events surrounding Jesus's birth, only two of these Gospel writers (Matthew and Luke) even mentioned such events; and having done so—as Albert Schweitzer had already noticed before he reached the age of ten—they totally left the participants—wise men and shepherds—out of the rest of the story. After presenting these worshipers as amazed, delighted, entranced, and even brought to salvation by the birth of Jesus, the Gospel writers forgot about them. To add to this problem, Luke depicts Jesus at the age of ten as astounding the doctors of the Jerusalem Temple with his learning and insight; yet none of these doctors, if Luke is to be believed, seemed remotely to have followed up such a remarkable boy.

Such problems fascinated and perplexed Schweitzer, as well as the German theologians of the nineteenth century. These men proved brilliant enough to tackle the subject in new ways and to suggest original, perhaps frightening (but certainly plausible) answers to the problems.

Their initial task, in the light of the contradictions in the four Gospels, seemed obvious enough: to decide which Gospel was written first, since (they deduced) the earliest ought to be the most reliable. Confronting this task, most of these theologians decided that the Fourth Gospel, that of John, stood apart, as a kind of poetic meditation on the meaning of Jesus's life, rather than a straightforward piece of historical biography.

The other three Gospels, Matthew, Mark, and Luke, seemed to give a much clearer synopsis of Jesus's life, his death, and his possible resurrection. From the word *synopsis*, these theologians decided to describe them as the "synoptic Gospels," and the synoptic problem involved the questions of how they were related to each other, whether one or two had been copied from one or more of the others, and above all, which was written first. Such questions frightened the ultraorthodox, who preferred to close their eyes to the problems involved. Such ultraorthodox Christians later were to persecute Schweitzer himself. But the difficulties they refused to acknowledge were faced head-on by a few Catholic theologians and above all by the great German Protestant theologians. These were devout men who, in spite of their piety, did not sacrifice scholarship on the altar of devotion. Such were the men whom Schweitzer recognized as making enormous leaps forward in one of the most central spiritual and intellectual quests of the Christian world. He was now privileged to sit at their feet.

Schweitzer indeed had the good fortune to go up to university when the rich German scholarship behind these audacious and exceedingly fruitful leaps forward in research and mankind's religious quest were producing undreamed-of fruits. Naturally enough, since these exhilarating developments in religious insight and intellectual venture were also terrifying to many of the more conservative faithful, some of the theologians he now came into contact with (and grew to revere) were already dubbed heretics—at the worst, thrown out of their university posts, often denied clerical livings, almost always execrated and denounced. All were inevitably far from orthodox, even heterodox, though not one of them wished to regard himself as a heretic. Some of them, reviled by the less adventurous, magnificently fought back against their timorous, if often learned, critics.

Virtually all of these theologians remained committed to following the pattern of life set by Jesus. It was for this reason that they passionately sought to uncover his true essence and the elusive facts of his historical existence. Schweitzer's own quest for the historical Jesus was inspired by a similar devotion. He too needed inspiration and sought it in an unknown Jesus. As Karl Budde, one of Schweitzer's brilliantly provocative teachers, put it when lecturing in the United States, "It has pleased God to give His human children the noblest and most beautiful flower of His revelation, the Gospel of His Son Jesus Christ." The problem was to redefine that revelation and to rediscover that Gospel.

So these Protestant Christians in late-nineteenth-century Germany perilously yet successfully combined a readiness to question everything with the inner conviction that somehow the results of their profoundly disturbing research would vindicate the Christian vision of Jesus. In Schweitzer the result was bizarre: eventually he decided both that Jesus as a man had been deluded and that he, Albert Schweitzer, must nevertheless follow the call of this deluded man.

Among the most searching and radical of these German Protestant theologians, two of the finest taught Schweitzer at Strasbourg. Some of his other teachers were scarcely less brilliant, learned, and provocative. At the end of October 1893, Schweitzer became a student at the university, living in a theological college presided over by the learned Pastor Alfred Erichson—not one of the daring speculators, though a scholar of enormous repute (and some boredom) who was completing at that time his magisterial edition of the works of the Reformer John Calvin.

Alongside the audacious geniuses of Strasbourg, such dogged scholars as Erichson also played their part in enhancing the renown of this superb university. Strasbourg was a new university, scarcely twenty years old, set up by the Germans after the Franco-Prussian War left Alsace in their hands. They had combined the old Catholic university set up by the Jesuits in the sixteenth century with the Lutheran university of 1621, providing their new foundation with sumptuous buildings and endowments that attracted the finest scholars. In consequence, as Albert Schweitzer himself boasted, when he reached the place as a student, "Strasbourg university was at the height of its reputation. Unhampered by tradition, teachers and students alike strove to realize the ideal of a modern university. There were hardly any professors of advanced age on the teaching staff. A fresh breeze of youthfulness penetrated everywhere."

Schweitzer was still anxious about his command of languages. Would he pass or fail the preliminary examination in Hebrew? By now, however, he had learned that brutal determination which was later to overcome nearly every seemingly impossible obstacle. He felt that his first term was spoiled by having to work for the Hebrew exam, which he passed after much effort the following February. Since he was still comparatively poor, he lived sparsely, drinking Alsatian beer instead of wine, from time to time relaxing at a Wagner concert or playing Bach at the church of Saint-Guillaume. He went everywhere by bicycle. When he needed money for a train ticket to Bayreuth, Schweitzer cut his food down to one meal a day. And pass he did.

The strain of his first year did not prevent the young student from zealously attending the lectures of Heinrich Julius Holtzmann, Wilhelm Windelband, and Theobald Ziegler. Professors Windelband and Ziegler lectured on the history of philosophy, a subject later to become dear to their young pupil. But Holtzmann was precisely the sparkling, mature, yet innovative theologian that Schweitzer really needed to encounter.

Just entering his sixties, Heinrich Julius Holtzmann was one of the older professors at Strasbourg when he began to teach Albert Schweitzer. He was also the foremost New Testament scholar of his time. After studying in Berlin, he had become a pastor in Baden before teaching at the University of Heidelberg from 1858 to 1874 and then moving to Strasbourg. At Heidelberg he had achieved his greatest scholarly insight: an almost impregnable proof that of the first three Gospels setting out the life of Jesus, the one that was written first happened not to be that of Matthew (the view supported both by its foremost position in the Christian Bible and by all subsequent Christian tradition), but the shortest Gospel of all, that of Mark. In addition, Holtzmann argued, Mark's outline of Jesus's life is the one that underlies those of the gospels of Matthew and Luke. Matthew and Luke copied Mark. They copied and embroidered him. He was their primary source.

Holtzmann believed (probably rightly) that Matthew had other sources besides Mark, in particular an earlier and therefore important collection of the sayings of Jesus. To Luke he gave less credence, regarding his Gospel as deriving largely from Matthew and Mark. But ultimately he believed that we must turn to Mark to discover the vital, life-enhancing truth about the historical Jesus.

At this time, many scholars found such contentions astounding, and scarcely anyone allowed the virtues of Holtzmann's conclusions until the evidence and his own cogent arguments drove them reluctantly to agree. Agree they almost all did. Schweitzer, already almost completely his own man, having learned all he could from Holtzmann, eventually did not agree, even though, in the words of W. G. Kümmel (the leading twentieth-century expert in this field), Holtzmann's work was quite simply "magnificent."

Albert Schweitzer sat at this magnificent theologian's feet. Holtzmann persuaded him to put in for a theological scholarship, worth twelve hundred marks a year over six years, which Schweitzer won, on the condition that when those six years were over he would take a degree in theology. Yet adoring and admiring Holtzmann as he did, the argumentative, shy, stubborn Gunsbach youth still deployed that independent intellectual streak he had displayed as a boy. He himself came to believe (almost certainly erroneously) that Matthew's Gospel was the first to be written. But at the age of twenty he was bright enough to recognize that he now was in the presence of a teacher whose lectures and seminars were on no account to be missed.

The lectures of other Strasbourg professors were almost as precious to the rapidly maturing Albert. Obliged from April 1, 1894, to suffer a year of conscripted military service, he made friends with his captain and agreed to a pact enabling him to reach university almost every day to hear Professor Windelband's 11:00 A.M. lectures. But in Schweitzer's eyes, Heinrich Julius Holtzmann reigned supreme. When autumn came, Schweitzer's military unit was ordered on maneuvers near Hochfelden in Lower Alsace. Mindful of Holtzmann, conscript Albert put a Greek New Testament in his haversack, in order "to avoid disgracing myself in the eyes of a tutor whom I respected so much." At the beginning of the winter term, theological students competing for a scholarship were normally obliged to sit an examination in three subjects, but those doing military service took only one. Significantly, Albert chose to sit the exam in one of Holtzmann's two specialties: the synoptic Gospels.

Not that Holtzmann's other specialty did not also fascinate him. Far from content with advancing one audacious (and almost certainly correct) hypothesis about the roots of Christianity, Holtzmann had turned secondly to what was potentially a yet more contentious aspect of the life of Jesus: the psychological makeup of the Christian Savior. This too was something Albert Schweitzer deeply imbibed. Whereas prevailing Christian orthodoxy perceived Jesus as always in command of his destiny and his own emotions, Holtzmann boldly divided Jesus's public and psychological life in two. First, he maintained, Jesus had experienced a period of virtually unsullied success, which climaxed at Caesarea Philippi when his disciple Peter declared him to be the Messiah, the longed-for Jewish Chosen One. Next, and almost immediately, Jesus went through a period of miserable failure, in which he increasingly conceived himself not as the mighty one but as a suffering servant, brought low by his heavenly father on behalf of his fellow human beings.

Such speculations were by no means the product of an overheated imagination. Undergirding them were Holtzmann's earlier studies on the problem of which was the earliest Gospel. Grant that Saint Mark's came first, and all subsequent theology had to take into account (as Holtzmann did) the extraordinary change of emphasis Mark's Gospel displays after Peter's confession at Caesarea Philippi that, in his view, Jesus is the Messiah. At that moment, Jesus forbids his followers to reveal this view of him to anyone. Holtzmann's psychologizing of Jesus was no mere speculation. This exceptional professor transmitted to Albert Schweitzer the conception of basing new and richly rewarding approaches to the significance of Jesus not on fantasy, but on solid scholarship.

Again much here frightened contemporary Christian believers who approached the Bible with the view that Jesus had somehow descended from heaven with a ready-made, immutable gospel, one authoritatively given to him by his father in heaven. By contrast, Heinrich Julius Holtzmann presented a Jesus whose own consciousness progressively developed like that of any other human being. Holtzmann did not offer this view as some sort of heresy. He devoutly believed, first, that Jesus's own self-understanding moved him toward a deepening conviction that he was indeed the longed-for Jewish Messiah. Second, he did not doubt that Jesus's conviction was true.

Albert Schweitzer greatly admired this aspect of Holtzmann's teaching. Holtzmann's own portrait of what he regarded as the true Jesus was brief, but it entranced Schweitzer as it did many others:

> The way in which Holtzmann exhibited [his own concept of Jesus] was so perfect, so artistically charming.... Scarcely ever had a description of the life of Jesus exercised so irresistible an influence as that short outline—it embraces scarcely twenty pages—[with] which Holtzmann closes his examination of the synoptic Gospels. This chapter became the creed and catechism of all who handled the subject during the following decades.

At the close of the nineteenth century, Schweitzer perceived that although Holtzmann never adequately wrote this ideal life of Jesus, with his short sketch of the public ministry of Jesus, his critically detailed examination of all the available sources, and his full account of what Jesus taught he yet provided "the plan and the prepared building material, so that anyone can carry out the construction in his own way and on his own responsibility." Schweitzer eventually did that very thing. For Schweitzer's own vision of the life of Jesus, Holtzmann had provided the bricks. Schweitzer produced the cement and mortar to construct his personal building. Though no less heterodox, it turned out to be powerfully different from Holtzmann's.

Even as a student Schweitzer had possessed the necessary gall to begin to probe his renowned teacher's possible shortcomings. Albert did not at that time possess enough gall to acquaint Holtzmann with this fact. On army maneuvers he began to question his master. During the summer of 1894, Holtzmann remembered, this vigorous young Albert "did not know what fatigue was." Although in the autumn his army service was seriously interrupting his university life, he still very much needed to win a scholarship in order to continue his theological and philosophical studies without serious penury. Having chosen to be examined in his professor's pet subject, the synoptic Gospels, he strenuously devoted himself both to military maneuvers and to intense New Testament study.

Discovering that he no longer wholeheartedly agreed with his professor, Schweitzer now went farther along his own tracks. Scrutinizing and assiduously comparing the three synoptic Gospels, he read in the tenth and eleventh chapters of Matthew's Gospel the most perplexing statements, none of which seemed to derive from the supposed earliest text, the Gospel of Mark.

First, in the tenth chapter of Matthew's Gospel Jesus tells his closest followers to expect severe persecution almost immediately. But nothing of the kind happens. In spite of the divine prediction, they simply are not persecuted. Equally bizarre, Jesus then tells them to expect that the heavenly kingdom of the Jewish Messiah (the "Son of man," God's Chosen One) will come about before they have traveled through all the cities of Israel. Again, this doesn't happen.

"How does it come about," Schweitzer asked, "that Jesus leads his followers to expect events about which the rest of the narrative is silent?" Schweitzer's uncompromising conclusion was that Jesus had been mistaken. "The bare text compelled me to assume that Jesus really announced persecution for the disciples and, as a sequel to this, the immediate appearance of the heavenly Son of man, and that Jesus's announcement was shown by subsequent events to be wrong," Schweitzer decided. His conclusion forced him even further into the fearful task of trying to delve into Jesus's psychology. Schweitzer now asked, "How did Jesus come to entertain such an expectation, and what must his feelings have been when events turned out otherwise than he had assumed they would?"

To make the question even more traumatic for a devout son of a Protestant household who had so much identified with his mentor Heinrich Julius Holtzmann, Schweitzer felt obliged to disagree profoundly with his revered professor's answer to these questions. Holtzmann, with his insistence on the primacy of Mark's Gospel, offered the explanation that the tenth chapter of Matthew was not in truth a historical discourse at all. The historical Jesus had never uttered the prophecies there attributed to him. After his death, later followers had devoutly made them up, creating the chapter out of various "sayings of Jesus" preserved in the Christian tradition.

Albert Schweitzer found the explanation wholly inadequate, indeed incomprehensible. Jesus's later followers would have been fools, he reasoned, to invent such an implausible speech for their master and lord. As Schweitzer succinctly put it, "A later generation would never have gone so far as to put into Jesus's mouth words which were belied by the subsequent course of events."

The bit now between his teeth, Albert Schweitzer rushed headlong into the next chapter of Matthew's Gospel. Here Jesus's cousin John sent some of his disciples to Jesus with a question. This John had made a powerful impact on the many members of the local Jewish community by preaching that the supernatural kingdom of God was about to break into and overpower the world. To prepare men and women for this coming, he had started baptizing them in the river Jordan, washing their sins away so to speak. Now John asked Jesus whether he was "the one who is to come."

Schweitzer pondered the question. What did John mean by "the one who is to come"? Did he mean the Jewish Messiah himself? Or was he referring to someone else, the ancient Jewish prophet Elijah, whom many Jews believed would rise from the dead just before the coming of the Messiah, in order to proclaim the Messiah's imminent arrival?

According the the eleventh chapter of Matthew's Gospel, Jesus replied to this question not to John but to his own disciples. John the Baptist, he said, was Elijah. So, Schweitzer concluded, Jesus had not understood John's question to mean "Are you the Messiah?" but "Are you Elijah, risen from the dead?" If the account in Matthew's Gospel is at all accurate, Schweitzer reasoned, the conclusion could only be that Jesus supposed himself to be the Messiah, with John the Baptist as Elijah, his forerunner.

Yet this conclusion raised yet another major question. If Jesus was the Messiah and knew it, why at this point did he not directly and openly proclaim the fact in response to John the Baptist's question? The problem, Schweitzer sardonically observed, embarrassed most commentators. Some weakly decided that Jesus was testing John the Baptist's faith, a solution nowhere hinted at in Matthew's Gospel itself. To add to the perplexity, Jesus had made further comments about John, in particular that of all those born of women he was the greatest, but that the least person in the kingdom of heaven was greater than he.

Preachers and commentators of the time had been used to explaining this remark by arguing that Jesus was placing John at a lower level than his own disciples. The explanation, Schweitzer thought, was both "unsatisfying and crude." Were not all of Jesus's disciples (and Jesus himself) "born of women?" He turned to Jesus's phrase "the kingdom of heaven." The difference between John and the least person in the kingdom of heaven, Schweitzer mused, surely lay in the fact that the latter now lived in a supernatural condition, in heaven, akin to the angels. John might well be the greatest man that ever appeared in the natural realm; those living in the supernatural realm, however humble, were bound to be greater than he.

So Albert Schweitzer approached a momentous conclusion, finally formulated when he reached home after his army maneuvers. He had become certain that "Jesus had announced no kingdom that was to be founded and realized in the natural world by himself and those who believed in him. Instead he had announced a kingdom that would come almost immediately, as the new supernatural age dawned."

Now Schweitzer's earlier shyness transformed itself into a courteous (and wisely calculated) diffidence. As he later recalled, "I should of course have regarded it as an impertinence to hint to Holtzmann in my examination which occured a very short time later that I was far from convinced by the conception of the life of Jesus which he put forward and which was universally accepted by contemporary critical theologians." The caution is judicious; the presumption is audacious. The young student, approaching only his first vital university examination, is taking on the whole of late-nineteenth-century Protestant scholarship and, in particular, the apogee of German theology. Yet he keeps his views to himself.

Did Holtzmann realize the quality of the young man he was teaching? The evidence certainly points this way. He made sure that Albert Schweitzer, his studies hampered by military service, passed the examination with ease. Instead of relentlessly grilling the wayward, brilliant undergraduate, Heinrich Julius Holtzmann gently interviewed him for twenty minutes and simply asked him to summarize the contents of the first three Gospels.

German universities in those days did not tie their students down to a dully rigorous course of study. During his remaining years at Strasbourg, Albert Schweitzer, without risking his academic career, was able to occupy himself with the study of the synoptic Gospels, often at risk to the other subjects in the faculties of philosophy and theology. But he also found a teacher even more congenial to him than the tantalizingly profound Holtzmann: an Old Testament specialist named Karl Budde. Few could dislike Budde. On Budde's arrival at Strasbourg, Professor Holtzmann immediately welcomed his younger colleague. Not long after the two men left Strasbourg for the University of Marburg. The two men were soon collaborating on an edition of Eduard Reuss's *Briefwechsel mit seinem Schüler und Freunde Karl Heinrich Graf* (Giessen 1904).

Schweitzer, already entranced that he was in a university for the most part staffed (apart from Heinrich Julius Holtzmann) by the enthusiastic young, warmed tremendously to the new professor, who was still not yet fifty years old. Born at Bensberg near Cologne on April 13, 1850, Karl Ferdinand Reinhardt Budde had been educated at the universities of Bonn, Berlin, and Utrecht. Arriving at Strasbourg in 1879 as an associate professor, scarcely a few months had elapsed before he became a full professor.

As few dons outside German universities do, Budde displayed a dazzling command of languages as well as a gift for communicating abstruse arguments to intelligent laymen and -women who were motivated to interpret and learn about their spiritual heritage. As a result, Karl Budde was welcomed as a visiting lecturer both in Britain and in the United States. He also brought to the savagely intellectual world of German theology some of the charm and grace of British, French, and American religious speculation, translating for example the celebrated 1882 Gifford lectures on *Natural Religions and Universal Religions* (as *Volkereligion und Weltreligion*, Berlin 1883). In 1898 he gave a series of lectures on the religion of Israel as far as the exile in the finest theological seminaries and universities of the United States that made his name as a leading European religious savant. As the Americans noted, he lectured "in excellent English."

If Albert Schweitzer later appeared to be a universal genius, expounding music, religion, philosophy, and such practical skills as how to build a jungle hospital, his favorite university professor set him a similar example. Budde not only lectured throughout the western scholarly world on his own discipline, he also incidentally produced a highly praised biography and catalog of the works of the graphic artist and painter Adrian Ludwig Richter. "His books on Richter's art are most distinguished, and his great Richter collection in the Museum at Essen is acclaimed as wonderful by experts," wrote one critic. The prolific Budde was still doggedly writing scarcely two weeks before his death in January 1935. Schweitzer and his mentor were similarly prolific.

Small wonder that Schweitzer loved the man. Curiously enough, both men had been obliged partly to suspend their theological studies to join the army, in Budde's case by serving on the German side in the Franco-Prussian War of 1870–71. None of Budde's distractions, military or artistic, prevented him from separating from the first five books of the Bible—books specially sacred to the Jews—a crucial element known as the Yahwistic tradition, a series of texts in which God is given a unique name and regarded as supreme above all others. Old Testament scholars still build upon the foundations Budde laid.

Karl Budde, like Heinrich Julius Holtzmann, was both a daring pioneer in biblical criticism and a devout believer. He had no truck with the many Christians who, at that time, wished to maintain that every word of the whole corpus of biblical literature was an equally inspired and authentic revelation of God's will for mankind. He still looked upon Jesus as his Lord. He still regarded the Old Testament as embodying the word of God. At the same time, he believed that the deepest eternal truths were here contained in earthen vessels.

So Budde was ready to make incisive value judgments about the views of the Jewish sages and prophets whose words, deeds, and writings were recorded in his beloved Hebrew Bible. At the same time, as his pupil Albert Schweitzer endeavored to do (and not just with the various strands of Judaism, but with all the world's religions), Karl Budde wanted to see every part of this spiritual inheritance integrated in one sublime whole. "Can we conceive of any sharper contrasts than we find between the world-wide, glowing universalism of Deutero-Isaiah and the narrow, icy particularism of Ezekiel—between the ritualism of Ezekiel and the complete superiority of Jeremiah and Deutero-Isaiah to all external cult—between the resignation of Jeremiah and the enthusiastic expectations of the other two—between the inner life of God in Jeremiah and the world-wide sublimity of the God of Ezekiel?" he asked, nonetheless adding, "And yet they all belong to the same people of Israel and became the three foundation pillars on which post-exilic Judaism raised itself anew."

From his teaching Albert Schweitzer learned to appreciate Judaism as a profound synthesis of many diverse elements. Karl Budde claimed that, "The phantom of the rigid uniformity of the religion of Israel has dissolved before our eyes. In its beginnings this religion had developed out of the most heterogeneous elements; a mass of different heathen religions had to furnish their contributions to it. And at the close of Israel's independent existence we find three prophetic figures, sprung from the bosom of the same people, who confess the same God and yet seem to proclaim three fundamentally different religions." Schweitzer himself was later to set about attempting to create an even profounder synthesis of all the great religions of the world.

Albert Schweitzer confessed that he experienced the lectures of this genius as "an artistic delight." What especially pleased him, he declared, was Karl Budde's "simple yet thorough method of expounding intellectually sound conclusions." We may legitimately speculate more: In later life Albert Schweitzer would infuriate many people by holding, at one and the same time, apparently diametrically opposed views. Obviously, his own often tormented psyche partly explains this. But the complex, scholarly insights of his highly emotional brain derived some of their cogency from the long-forgotten Professor Karl Budde, a lecturer who, in his time, gave invaluable sustenance to Albert Schweitzer and to countless others. While never eschewing either his own Christian faith or his profound scholarly integrity, Budde could at once clinically dissect the Old Testament and regard its essence as of eternal value for the human race.

A third friend among Schweitzer's professors was Theobald Ziegler. As a theologian, Ziegler greatly admired the writings of David Friedrich Strauss, who had published a life of Jesus in 1835 and been hounded from a university teaching post because of it. Ziegler regarded 1835 as "the great revolutionary year of modern theology." Mindful of Strauss's fate, he was perhaps wise to switch in later years from the study of theology to that of philosophy. He persuaded his student to take up the study of Kant, and to do so at the Sorbonne under the guidance, among others, of the brilliant modernist scholar Auguste Sabatier. So, in the autumn of 1898 at the age of twenty-three, Schweitzer arrived in Paris and rented a tiny room at no. 20 in the rue de Sorbonne. Schweitzer's thesis professes to have found many contradictions in Kant's thought and, paradoxically, insists that Kant was a genius precisely because he attempted to unify these because, having voiced them, he never felt them. When he presented his thesis to Ziegler the following March, the professor was delighted, exclaiming, "A new philosophical genius has risen amongst us."

The writings of one other heterodox genius aroused Albert Schweitzer's enthusiasm while he was a student, namely those of the Berlin professor Adolf von Harnack. Schweitzer had four months' grace before his viva examination in philosophy. He decided to spend the time in Berlin. He rented another little room, this time a third-story flat in Kochstrasse. Its doorway (as he wrote to his goddaughter Suzi) was huge, set between a general store and a bookshop, but one had to be careful not to step on the feet of the pipe-smoking porter upon entering. Schweitzer apparently longed for Alsatian wine to supplement his Berlin beer and begged Suzi to help his father bottle some for him.

Soon he had entered the social and intellectual life of the university, helped by an introduction into the household of Frau Curtius, the widow of a great classical scholar whose stepson was the district superintendent of Colmar. Schweitzer revered other great teachers in Berlin besides Harnack, but Harnack was such a phenomenally learned church historian and theologian that he usually rendered the young student speechless. He used to quote Goethe's dictum, "If anyone restricts his life to his own experience alone, he is like an animal in meager pasture, tethered by an evil spirit so that it can move only in a restricted circle and cannot see the rich green meadows surrounding it." The whole of human spiritual and intellectual achievement was Harnack's green pasture. "We must—like Faust—enlarge our own ego into the ego of the world," he proclaimed. "This is done by appropriating with noble appetite the whole course of history and all its great and good personalities, and by making them extensions of one's own essence."

If Albert Schweitzer became renowned as a polymath, his mentor and, later, friend Harnack was a yet greater one. His father had become professor of pastoral theology at Dorpat in Estonia, and Harnack himself had been a professor at Leipzig, Giessen, and Marburg before coming to Berlin in 1889. By then he had made himself master of virtually every piece of early Christian literature, editing and publishing a vast corpus of material, writing on monasticism, and finally producing a three-volume history of Christian dogma stretching from the earliest days of the church to the Reformation.

Harnack's huge brain was equal to the task of extending his own personality by empathizing with the great personalities of human history; and at the center of the whole saga he perceived Jesus as the greatest and best personality of all. But which Jesus? Certainly not the one being preached in John's gospel, a Son of God preexistent in heaven before his actual birth on earth. As early as 1873 Harnack confessed privately that he had ceased to believe the doctrine of Jesus's preexistence. Among Schweitzer's teachers, Heinrich Julius Holtzmann and Karl Budde had been heterodox enough; in the eyes of many contemporaries, Adolf von Harnack seemed a scandalous heretic.

Harnack believed there was a distinction to be traced even in the New Testament between the teaching *of* Jesus and teaching *about* Jesus. The first he described as "the joyous news to the poor, the peaceable, the meek and the pure in heart, the news that God's kingdom is near, that it will soothe sorrows and anxiety, bring justice and establish man's childhood in God in addition to giving all good things. It is a new order of life, above the world and politics."

New Testament teaching *about* Jesus, on the other hand, seemed to Harnack to have led to immense and regrettable distortions of the true faith, to a needlessly dogmatic Christianity, and to profitless sectarianism. This dogmatic teaching included the assertion that God had devised a plan for redeeming mankind by means of the incarnation of Jesus as the Son of God. It included the concept of Jesus's crucifixion as a ransom for all mankind. It comprised the concept of his resurrection, his "conquest of the devil," and the development of all this in Pauline theology as further parts of a divine scheme of salvation. It led to the erroneous notions found in the early church about the imminent coming of God's kingdom.

Here, then, was a theologian whose example Albert Schweitzer could follow in sitting lightly on Christian dogma while still holding fast, for the rest of his life, to what he regarded as the essence of Jesus's gospel. Schweitzer's Jesus, though tragically deluded above all in supposing that his crucifixion would bring about the kingdom of God, was still a Jesus whose call must be obeyed. "He sets us to the tasks which he has to fulfil in our time. He commands. And to those who obey him, whether they be wise or simple, He will reveal himself."

Schweitzer and Harnack became firm and lifelong friends. The last letter Harnack ever wrote was to Schweitzer. They had much in common. Both men were the sons of Lutheran pastors; both were academics; both suffered deeply from the barbs of contemporary Christians.

Harnack's three-volume history of Christian dogma was a monumentally learned book, yet it was written out of deep passion, even torment. When the first volume appeared, Harnack wrote to a friend of his happiness at being able, at last, to write what he truly thought instead of appearing to the world as someone other than he really was. "In the strength of this joy," he hoped, "all the tortures that I have endured will vanish." He was wrong. Again like Albert Schweitzer, in the search for religious truth he suffered continual abuse. Schweitzer himself came to believe that this was one sure way of knowing he was truly following Jesus. Jesus, he wrote, "will reveal himself to his followers in the toils, the conflicts and the sufferings which they shall pass through in his fellowship."

Both men were also children of the Protestant Reformation. This Reformation, Harnack taught, had begun to separate the essence of Christianity from the dogmatic structures surrounding and stifling it. In the fourth century after the founding of Christianity, this dogma, he argued, had become an overwhelmingly authoritative doctrinal system. From around that time, Harnack concluded, the church was never again completely sincere—always professing more than it could defend, carry out, or believe. Harnack perceived the chief task of Christian scholarship in his own time as the completion of the work of the sixteenth-century Reformers in unstripping the essence of Jesus's teaching from this intolerable, unnecessary dogmatic burden. He saw it as a crucially important mission, vital for the survival of

Christianity. If the church would only accept the insights of the Reformation, of modern science, of Kant, and the Enlightenment, he wrote, she must confess openly that "in the worship of God no-one is forced to profess things he has no need to profess."

Getting back to the essential Jesus involves, according to Harnack, five major intellectual tasks. First, it requires an uncovering of the original sources, both of the gospel and of the dogmas that Harnack believed had stifled it—hence his brilliantly laborious publication of text after text. Next, it demands a scientific history that sets aside all metaphysical speculation. Third, to discover doggedly the true facts of history is a sacred duty involving a commitment of the heart as well as the head. Fourth, the church historian must connect every institution arising in the development of Christianity with the spiritual impulse that had helped to produce it. Finally, the task of religious history is to expound and analyze the every cultural factor shaping each historical event. Few scholars have ever possessed the mental equipment to cope with more than one of these five tasks. Harnack coped stupendously with them all.

Everyone, including Schweitzer, acknowledged his brilliance. Many, not including Schweitzer, were also enraged by his conclusions. What made this remarkable scholar so controversial was the judgmental way in which he interpreted the development of the Christian faith. Throughout his *History of Dogma* Harnack attempted to show that the metaphysical aspects of Christian theology were an alien element, derived from Greek philosophy rather than the simple message of Jesus. From the earliest times, he argued, Christianity had become intermingled with Hellenism. As a result, habits of Greek thought brought into Christianity much inessential dogma which, Harnack insisted, every scholar and believer was required to criticize. From him, Schweitzer derived a savagely critical spirit in his own quest for the historical Jesus. As for Harnack, his own view went so far as to maintain that for a true Protestant, dogma ought not to exist at all.

Such views infuriated orthodox Protestants as well as, if not even more than, Catholics. Harnack's mother told him that his *History of Dogma* stabbed Harnack's father in the heart. It upset other people too. When in December 1887 the faculty of theology at Berlin unanimously proposed him for the vacant chair of church history, the conservative church authorities did their utmost to block Harnack's appointment on the grounds that he was evasive when it came to accepting the miracles recounted in the Gospels; that his writings were destructive of the New Testament canon; and that he was heterodox on the biblical witness to the doctrine of the Trinity. After nine months of fracas, the newly enthroned Kaiser Wilhelm II cut through the controversy, overrode the objections, and decreed that Harnack should be appointed. This, then, was yet another dangerously speculative theologian whose genius Schweitzer had recognized and whose views, like Schweitzer's own, brought him "torment."

Soon, reluctantly but inevitably, Harnack was plunged into another controversy that was not only splitting the Prussian church but soon would affect Schweitzer himself: who was theologically fit to be ordained? Should all candidates for the ministry have to acknowledge the truth of the Apostles' Creed? Naturally, Harnack said no. The Apostles' Creed, he argued with sophistication, contained, on the one hand, too little to form the basis of an intelligent faith. On the other hand, some of the Creed was superfluous to Christianity. Harnack wanted a shorter but more rational statement, which every candidate for ordination should thenceforth rigorously be obliged to accept. Such were the passions aroused by this controversy, and so influential was Harnack, that when he set out his views in writing in 1892, the resulting book went through twenty-seven editions in four years.

For his part, Albert Schweitzer relished such controversies and deeply admired Harnack's courageous stand. Schweitzer's own background and family heritage involved every side in the arguments. As he put it, "My grandfather was rationalist, my father a religious liberal and my great uncle and aunt staunchly orthodox." Only Harnack's monumental learning at first over-awed him, and thus temporarily delayed the development of their deep friendship.

Yet Schweitzer never totally agreed with Harnack's distillation of the essence of Christianity. For Schweitzer, Harnack was hoist by his own petard. His own version of "true Christianity" was culturally conditioned, fitting all too easily into his own worldview—that of a late-nineteenth-century German Lutheran. Harnack made Jesus in his own image. And, in Schweitzer's view, he was not quite radical enough when he began stripping the dogma away from the historical Jesus. Harnack, he judged, "almost entirely ignores the contemporary limitations of Jesus's teaching. He starts out with a gospel which carries him down without difficulty to the year 1899." Albert Schweitzer perceived in the New Testament a far stranger, far more mysterious Jesus than Harnack did.

Schweitzer was sufficiently radical to go beyond even the drastic historical scrupulousness of his mentor. And like his mentor, he was soon to be persecuted for his own extreme, laudable, and devout scrupulousness. For the time being, however, life seemed good. In August 1899 he returned to Strasbourg from the social whirl of Berlin having done insufficient work on Kant. His examiners, led by Ziegler, proved lenient at the viva. Schweitzer was granted his degree.

CHAPTER 5

◆

The Impossible Demands
of Jesus

O f all the cities of France, Schweitzer most adored Colmar. His first visit to Paris in October 1893 coincided with a flamboyant parade of Russian *matelots* in that city; to him it was nothing compared with the cavalcade of Colmar. The Louvre could not compare, in his eyes, with the Colmar Museum, and its pictures, he thought, were far inferior to the celebrated works by Mathias Grünewald and Martin Schongauer housed in Alsace. Schweitzer, whose unruly hair never succumbed to a comb, particularly identified with a portrait by Grünewald of Saint John the Apostle, who displayed the same shaggy locks. "I too was afflicted with a head of hair continually in disorder," he exclaimed. "In the apostle St. John I discovered a fellow-companion in misfortune." Did the young Saint John, Schweitzer wondered, suffer the same misery as he had done each morning while a maid attempted to comb his impossible hair? Did people say to the young apostle what unkind adults said of Schweitzer as a boy: "His hair mimics his character" and "The locks lack discipline just as the boy does"? The Saint John of Mathias Grünewald, Schweitzer declared a half-century later, relieved him of his inferiority complex.

Here too Schweitzer made a fateful and apparently irrational decision. The Alsatian sculptor Frédéric-Auguste Bartholdi, who had gained an international reputation with his *Lion of Belfort* and the statue on Liberty Island in Upper New York Bay, had sculpted at Colmar a monument for Admiral Bruat. Its statues represented far-flung nations, and Schweitzer felt himself particularly drawn to that of a powerful black man. Contemplating this noble, suffering figure, he perceived a melancholy in his herculean face and began to reflect on the fate of black men and women in his own day. "His face, with its sad, thoughtful expression, spoke to me of the misery of the dark continent," Schweitzer recalled. Later he would declare, "If a record could be made of all that has happened between the white and the colored races, some of the pages—referring to recent as well as to earlier times—would be turned over unread, because their contents would be too horrible for the reader."

When his sister Louisa married Monsieur Jules Ehretsmann and went to live in Colmar, Schweitzer had frequent reason to visit the city. Each time, he purposely went to brood over Bartholdi's statue, in order, as he put it, to be "tête à tête with my negro." This statue evoked in him a vow that at the age of thirty he would devote himself to relieving the lot of the natives of Africa. His negro, he wrote, really lived on the Ivory Coast, and that was where he would serve him.

First, however, Schweitzer was destined for university and for national service. Although he was to remain an academic for eighteen years beginning in 1893, these were years of turmoil and interruption. Visits to Paris to study the philosophy of Kant and to perfect his technique as an organ scholar, military service, marriage, and the years he spent as principal of his college in Strasbourg were punctuated by the furor caused by his publications. Above all, a time bomb continued to tick away as the moment approached when Schweitzer would abandon his academic career to devote the rest of his life to the service of his fellow men and women.

Intellectually, these were heady times, and Schweitzer the student, his mustache trimmed but his hair unruly, smoking a fashionably long pipe, entered fully into them. "In those years of the ebbing century we students came to know the writings of Friedrich Nietzsche and Leo Tolstoy," he wrote. Both iconoclasts were still alive, and both by their writings instilled in Schweitzer the notion that a spiritual tiredness had gripped a generation that had once been so proud of its work and efficiency. Schweitzer considered Nietzsche's *Beyond Good and Evil* second in the brilliance of its style only to Luther's translation of the Bible, but he deplored its message. He was astounded that the leading religious thinkers and the philosophers of his day had so feebly responded to Nietzsche's attack on the moral values that had developed out of Greek philosophy and Christianity. Whereas Tolstoy said yes to an ethical system that included love and compassion, Nietzsche contended that these two moral values were the attributes of weak and timid spirits. "It was in this dramatic fashion that we, the youth of the passing century, had come face to face with two widely differing worldviews," Schweitzer recalled, adding that the few people who spoke out against Nietzsche seemed incapable of doing so effectively, for the foundation of their own moral values was not solid enough to prevail against him.

Schweitzer also was astonished at the general complacency of this era. "In looking back I could never understand the optimism over the achievements of the times," he wrote. "Everywhere, many seemed to suppose that we had not merely advanced in knowledge, but that we had reached heights in spirituality and ethics we had never attained before and would never lose." To him, on the contrary, it seemed that his generation not only had failed to surpass the spiritual life of past generations, but also that "we were really only nibbling from their accomplishments, and that, in many respects, our spiritual inheritance was dribbling out of our hands."

Increasingly, as he turned his attention to the civilization and ethics of the last decade of the nineteenth century, he became convinced of the need to make a thorough and critical study of the spiritual state of the times in which he lived. A spur to this ambition, and a tentative title for the work, appeared in the summer of 1900, which Schweitzer spent at the University of Berlin. There the widow of the great Greek classical scholar Ernst Curtius was in the habit of inviting academics to her afternoon coffee hours. One afternoon Schweitzer and Frau Curtius were joined by some members of the Prussian Academy of Sciences. In the middle of an animated discussion, one of them concluded his remarks with the words, "All we are, after all, are *epigones.*" The remark struck Schweitzer like lightning. "I was, then, not the only one who was aware of the fact that we were living in an era filled with bad imitators of the past—the epigones!" The young academic had a title for his projected critical study: *We Epigones* would characterize his era as one that unsuccessfully attempted to imitate a greater past.

We Epigones eventually would be written and published— though not under that title. But in the meantime, Schweitzer was to produce a far more iconoclastic work, a masterpiece which made his reputation, which would never be surpassed in any other of his writings, and which for a time threatened to brand him as an enemy of the Christianity he so devoutly espoused.

The religious passions of the early twentieth century centered remarkably on the personality of Jesus. Schweitzer, along with countless others, was driven to enunciate his own view of the founder of Christianity. What was his character? Was he God or man? And what relevance could he have for the twentieth century? As a pastor's son, and simply as a western Christian born in the late nineteenth century, Schweitzer had absorbed with his mother's milk the notion that the authentic words and fate of Jesus were of incalculable importance for life on earth and in the hereafter. He had also inherited the gravest doubts about that hereafter and about the authenticity of the traditional record of Jesus's words. Some extremists were even going so far as to doubt whether Jesus ever lived. Many doubted that he had risen from death. For a young theologian of Schweitzer's background and academic supremacy, it was inevitable that he attempt an answer to these problems.

His answer is short, precise enough, seductive, brilliant— but a sketch rather than a portrait. Renowned for his devotion to the Christian ideal and fascinated by the burgeoning impact of psychology and attempts to psychoanalyze Jesus, Schweitzer was never inspired to delineate at length the personality of his master. Schweitzer's complex personality at base was a unity; and it was toward the close of his medical studies in 1912 that he once again turned to study the character of the Jesus whose life he had hitherto, in his published writings, only briefly sketched.

All the while, however, Schweitzer had been preaching in the Church of Saint-Nicolas, Strasbourg, and these sermons reveal him grappling with the themes that would obsess him for the rest of his life. The central problem was the notion of the coming of the kingdom of God, a theme so crucial to Jesus's life and teaching that no follower of Jesus could ignore it. Yet in Schweitzer's view, it was an appalling stumbling block for modern believers. In 1912, expounding in the pulpit of Saint-Nicolas on Saint Paul's statement in his first letter to the Corinthians that "the kingdom of God is not a matter of talk, but of power," Schweitzer observed both that the words "kingdom of God" rang out like a bell and yet, at the same time, they signified something completely different for Jesus than they did for twentieth-century man.

Schweitzer was determined, come what may, to insist that the first Christians, including Jesus himself, expected the imminent end of the world. This was the major plank in his attack on the liberal Christian scholars of his own day.

He was, of course, not alone in coming to this conclusion. Toward the end of the nineteenth century and at the beginning of the twentieth the conclusion was dawning on scholars, particularly German ones, that current ways of reading the New Testament record were distorting one of its major thrusts. The leading critic to spot this was Johannes Weiss, whose ideas Schweitzer enthusiastically adopted and developed.

Although Schweitzer inevitably also made his own mistakes, his definitive insight remains unshakable: in reading the Bible one cannot separate the notion of the kingdom of God from a notion of the imminent end of the world. The insight inaugurated a century of wide-ranging Christian debate, in which widely different conclusions also were drawn.

The keyword was "eschatology." A Strasbourg scholar named Timothée Colani had introduced it into the debate as far back as 1864, in a study of Jesus and his Jewish background. For Colani, the term signified the last things, the final end of the created world. Colani believed he had identified three different eschatologies current during the earthly life of Jesus: the eschatology of the Jews at the time of Jesus; the eschatology of Jesus himself; and the eschatology of the primitive church. Then he asked a crucial question, namely, Which of the three was central to primitive Christianity?

In these eschatologies, the end of the created world was not seen as some slow running down or as a cataclysmic natural destruction, but depended on an act of God himself. Somehow, too, the earliest Christians had perceived Jesus as involved in bringing about the event. His words, his actions, his death, and eventually his apparent founding of a church were all seen as intimately bound up with the end of time.

Schweitzer's sudden realization that this was a central problem for twentieth-century as well as first-century Christians had occurred when, as a nineteen-year-old military conscript, he read and reread the tenth and eleventh chapters of the Gospel of Matthew in preparation for a preliminary examination in New Testament Greek. In these texts Jesus sent out his followers to preach the immediate arrival of the kingdom of God. They were to expect persecution, Jesus warned. He also told them that before they had preached to all the towns of Israel, the Son of man would have come with supernatural power. In short, Schweitzer realized, Jesus did not expect to see his disciples again.

Schweitzer put to himself two questions: How did Jesus come to this conclusion? And what was his reaction when his prophecy proved evidently false and the world did not come to an end? In an attempt to answer these questions, Schweitzer next devoured Heinrich Holtzmann's commentary on Matthew.

Under Holtzmann's influence, he developed a thesis from which he never basically swerved. Set out in principle in *The Secret of the Messiahship and Passion—A Sketch of the Life of Jesus,* a memoir published in 1901, Schweitzer's initial thesis was not even argued. The future theologian simply wrote five chapters of exposition. One attempted an analysis of the psychology of Jesus. The next set out Jesus's prophecy of the imminent arrival of the kingdom of God and his insistence that his own status as God's Messiah must be kept secret. Next he outlined the confrontation between Jesus and John the Baptist, before returning to the theme of the return of the disciples after their historic mission to Israel.

Schweitzer admitted that all our available sources of information about Jesus tell us nothing about his self-consciousness. "The evangelists have nothing to tell us about it, because Jesus told them nothing about it," is how Schweitzer later put this. Nonetheless, in spite of this complete lack of evidence, the last three chapters of his book offer an examination of the way Jesus kept secret his consciousness that he was the Messiah during the last years of his life on earth; they next expound the way he kept the messianic secret during his Passion; and finally they present a simple account of the whole life of the Master.

Five years later his monumental *Von Reimarus zur Wrede,* which was translated into English as *The Quest of the Historical Jesus,* appeared. In its last chapter Schweitzer set out his mature conclusions. Yet even here Schweitzer paid scant heed to any scholarly reservations others might display about his conclusions. Writing with serene self-confidence, he set out his thesis as one so self-evidently true that not a shadow of doubt or qualification appears. For this reason as much as for its intellectual cogency, Schweitzer's book became the paramount twentieth-century thesis about Jesus's self-consciousness and understanding of his own mission.

Jesus, Schweitzer insisted, was obsessed with the eschatological speculations of his contemporary Jews. The day when Yahweh would establish his kingdom was at hand. The sufferings of the time were an essential preliminary of that day. Soon

Satan and his allies would be conquered. And an essential cata-
lyst to all this was the appearance of the Son of man, after which
mankind would be judged—with some to be everlastingly
damned, others to be welcomed into eternal joy.

The role of Jesus in this process was central in Schweitzer's
analysis. Schweitzer remained skeptical about the relationship
between Jesus and John the Baptist, insisting that no one could
say with certainty whether they had ever met until John baptized Jesus in the river Jordan or that they even remained in contact afterwards. What seemed to Schweitzer certain was that,
from the moment of his baptism, Jesus was convinced of his own
messianic task. In his view, the kingdom of God was about to be
made supernaturally manifest. Already he believed himself to be
living the heavenly life. Moreover, Schweitzer postulated, Jesus
perceived that a special place was assigned in God's kingdom to
the lowly and the meek. Could the Messiah himself have been
born among the poor and humble?

At the same time, as Schweitzer fully knew, the Messiah was
traditionally conceived of as a descendant of King David. Again
and again in Matthew's Gospel Jesus is portrayed as the "son of
David." Sometimes he is simply described as such. As he rides
in triumph into Jerusalem, the crowds cry, "Hosanna to the son
of David." At other times, onlookers puzzle over his true identity. When Jesus heals a blind and dumb man, we read that "the
bystanders were all amazed, and the word went round, 'Can this
be the son of David?'" But the connection is made continually.

Yet throughout his ministry Jesus guards the secret of his
true identity. Schweitzer asks why and has no real answer, save
for the suggestion that Jesus feared to announce the coming of
God's kingdom with too great a show of certainty. Schweitzer
astonished not only his contemporaries but also subsequent theologians by declaring that even the preaching of this coming
kingdom lasted for, at most, a few weeks. The disciples were not
sent on a long mission to alert their fellow Jews to the imminent
arrival of the end of all things. Their preaching instead seems to
have been a token fulfillment of what Jesus saw as part of his
messianic destiny.

Here the tenth chapter of Matthew, pondered by the conscript Schweitzer, was crucial. "I tell you this," Jesus here informs his disciples, "before you have gone through all the towns of Israel the Son of man will have come." Yet the disciples return, their mission accomplished, and the kingdom of God has not yet come. Jesus's response was to abandon any hope of popular acclaim. Humiliation and suffering he now envisages as his certain lot, and the lot of his followers. "Be on your guard, for men will hand you over to their courts, they will flog you in their synagogues, and you will be brought before governors and kings for my sake, to testify before them and the heathen," he warns his disciples. "All will hate you for your allegiance to me, but the one who holds out to the end will be saved." Jesus is now preaching suffering as an essential preliminary to salvation. "No one is worthy of me who does not take up the cross and walk in my footsteps." Only by losing one's life will one gain eternal life.

The central nature of this insight inevitably led Schweitzer to ask what the significance of Jesus's own sufferings might have been in the whole drama of the last things. Jesus seemed to him now convinced that only after his own suffering would the kingdom of God come on earth. So Jesus sets off for Jerusalem not only to fulfill his own destiny, but also the destiny of the whole world. Schweitzer did not believe that the prophecies of his own death attributed to Jesus were authentic. They had, he held, been put into his mouth by later followers. But he did accept that during his trial Jesus had acknowledged that he was the Messiah and that soon he would be revealed as the Son of man, coming to announce the end of the world.

This startling thesis appears slightly less startling in the context of the scholarship of the time. Brilliant theologians had begun to ask how twentieth-century readers should interpret the New Testament—either as a series of documents imbued with contemporary Greek mysticism, or else as visions whose inspiration was essentially Jewish. Basically, for Schweitzer, the question was, from whence did Jesus derive these revolutionary ideas of the kingdom of God? In the 1880s, at Schweitzer's own splendid university, an Alsatian professor named Wilhelm Baldensperger had attempted to analyze the self-consciousness of Jesus in the light of the messianic hopes of his fellow Jews. But what brought the question of eschatology to the fore was the publication in 1892 of a book—a mere sixty-seven pages long— by the Göttingen savant Johannes Weiss on Jesus's preaching of the kingdom of God.

Drawing in part on the work of Baldensperger, Weiss concluded that Jesus had proclaimed that the final and inevitable arrival of the kingdom was imminent. The end would come suddenly and without warning. The battle with Satan had begun, and a new world was opening itself. This new world was not some human construct, brought about by man's slow enlightenment. In the thought of Jesus, it would happen simply and solely as the act of God. In the meantime, Jesus decided to conceal his own role in all this under the barely comprehensible title "Son of man."

The biblical basis of Weiss's thesis was incontrovertible. "Repent," said Jesus, "for the kingdom of Heaven is upon you." In Schweitzer's own beloved, puzzling tenth chapter of Matthew, Jesus is recorded urging his disciples to preach the same message. Saint Luke's Gospel records virtually the same proclamation. "When you come into a town," Jesus tells his messengers, tell the inhabitants that "the kingdom of God has come close to you." The same Gospel speaks of portents in the heavens and on earth which will soon indicate that the Son of man shall come in great glory. "When you see this happening," Jesus says, "you may know that the kingdom of God is near."

Taking up Weiss's thesis, Schweitzer fastened onto the brief period envisaged by the Gospels between Jesus's proclamation of repentance and the final coming of the kingdom. Heroic acts of self-sacrifice were demanded of Jesus's followers in that brief space of time, or interim. It was an era, Schweitzer assumed, of a special and particularly demanding "interim's ethic."

Schweitzer frequently complained that Weiss ought to have developed his thesis with greater rigor and certainly at greater length. Yet Schweitzer's own polemic—though undoubtedly carried out at much greater length than Weiss's—failed to surmount several crucial critical problems. One was that at the precise moment when he sat on a hillside doing national service and reading Matthew's Gospel, scholars were coming to the inescapable conclusion that this book, though the first in the New Testament, was not only written later than the Gospel of Mark but also leaned heavily upon it. Far from being the primary witness to the words and actions of Jesus, the author of Matthew used secondary sources for his narrative, and anyone seeking the closest witness we possess to Jesus's life must turn first to Mark.

Throughout his long life Schweitzer never accepted this reevaluation of the primary sources of the Christian faith. Matthew's Gospel remained for him the earliest of the four. As scholars increasingly began to see his crucial Chapter ten as a literary construction and not the uncontrovertible historical truth, Schweitzer was forced to one text in Mark's Gospel—Chapter 6, Verse 30—which declares that the disciples returned to their Master even though he had predicted that before their mission was complete the world would have ended.

Second, Schweitzer, against all the evidence, decided that the earthly mission of Jesus took at the most only a few months. Dogged scholars, putting together all the extant evidence of his activities and preaching, believe this can have been crammed into, at the least, three years. Third, whenever it suited him, Schweitzer was content to dismiss the biblical witness as legend, while at other times he took it to be the absolute truth. In doing so, he offered no criteria for determining why one testimony should be discarded and another accepted. The fact that Jesus apparently welcomed the return of his disciples and calmly carried on preaching is discounted in Schweitzer's analysis, even though the notion that the kingdom of God had not in fact arrived ought logically to have overwhelmed the Master.

Such considerations scarcely moved Schweitzer, simply because he was absolutely correct to confront the liberal theologians with their massive reconstruction of the Christian faith. Why had they for so long simply set aside the central eschatological element in the Gospels and in primitive Christianity? If Schweitzer magnified the eschatological aspects of the Gospels, he was publicly emphasizing an element that had been shamefully neglected.

Whatever different interpretations of the biblical texts might be considered legitimate, from the moment Albert Schweitzer's *Quest of the Historical Jesus* became a theological best-seller, never again could this central element in the Gospels' witness be set aside. The history of twentieth-century theological scholarship is littered with the attempts of British, German, and French theologians to come to terms with an uncomfortable aspect of Jesus's thinking—uncomfortable because it reveals the supposedly infallible Savior as decisively wrong in one central tenet of his preaching.

Many scholars attempted to close the gap between what Jesus expected and what happened by declaring that he was speaking the language of mythology, and that the imminent coming of the kingdom of God needed taking out of this realm and placing into, say, the realm of poetic truth. Others set about spiritualizing the notion of the kingdom of God, internalizing it in the hearts of men and women rather than allowing it a validity in the external world.

Schweitzer himself continually returned to the theme, adding new insights to those set out in his *Quest of the Historical Jesus.* Even as he was about to set out for Africa in 1913, he still found time to work on a new edition of his *Quest,* substantially developing several elements in the story. What he never abandoned was his initial insight that unless the notion of the imminent coming of God's kingdom is recognized as central to the preaching of Jesus, that message is inevitably distorted. It had, he also noted, been distorted throughout the Christian centuries.

War broke out one year later. The tribulations undergone by the missionary doctor and his wife during that conflict and in the immediate postwar years postponed any major attempt at setting out his profoundest conclusions in writing. Yet Schweitzer continued to be perplexed about the essential character of Jesus. Jesus still came to him, as he put it in his *Quest,* "as one unknown, without a name, as he came of old by the lakeside." Jesus, Schweitzer asserted, "came to men who knew him not." Insisting that they follow him, he set them tasks for their time, just as (Schweitzer believed) he was setting in the twentieth century new tasks. Only to those who obeyed his command would his essential character eventually be revealed—revealed, moreover, in their very obedience to his demands. "To those who obey him, be they wise or simple, he will reveal himself in the toils, the conflicts, the sufferings through which they shall pass in his company. As an ineffable mystery, they shall learn in their own experience who he is."

It would, therefore, have been a denial of this magisterial conclusion to Schweitzer's greatest book had he attempted to set out his own vision of Jesus without having undergone his own sufferings. But here Schweitzer does not let down his admirers. In 1950, his *Quest* was reprinted in a sixth edition, with a text identical to that of 1913 but with a new preface.

For thirty years Schweitzer had scarcely written about Jesus. Successive editions of the *Quest* had appeared without any new introduction or any revision. In August 1950, he suddenly produced a long preface for the sixth edition. Though silent for so long, he had remained preoccupied with the theme of his early manhood. At last he conceded that Jesus had introduced into the late Jewish notion of the kingdom of God a strong ethical emphasis on love. In doing so, "he charged the idea of the kingdom of God with those ethical forces with which we are now familiar."

Two years later, Schweitzer began work on a new book called *The Kingdom of God and Christianity*. His massive enterprise was to trace the notion of the kingdom of God from the days of the preexilic Jewish prophets as far as the time of the early church—and maybe even farther. Sailing from France to Gabon in May and June of 1951, he managed to finish the first four chapters. At Gunsbach he set about the rest. These chapters were never finished; but when the book appeared, two years after Schweitzer's death, seventy pages—a good third of the whole—were devoted to the notion of the kingdom in the preaching of

Jesus. Only after his death did Schweitzer finally speak as fully as he could of the man who had inspired his magisterial life.

In consequence, we can trace with clarity how Albert Schweitzer came to perceive in the Jesus described in the first three Gospels two essential elements that are continually at play: eschatology and ethics. The moral obligation that Schweitzer clearly experienced on contemplating the massive Colmar statue of a black man is scarcely visible here. The eschatological puzzles that had preoccupied Schweitzer in his earlier years remain. As many readers subsequently judged, eschatology, in Schweitzer's view of Jesus, was still swallowing up the Jesus who taught us the right way to lead our lives.

Such critics were wrong. Schweitzer was convinced to the end of his life that Jesus preached (in substantially the same fashion as many of his Jewish contemporaries) the imminent end of the world. Ethics was therefore inevitably subordinate to eschatology. Yet to preach the imminent end of the world posed for men and women not fatalism, but enormous ethical demands. They were summoned to repentance before the final judgment. An utterly new order of human affairs was about to be realized. In anticipation, even now men and women were obliged to respond to this new order by heroically living as if that state of affairs was already in being. The effort was heroic because in truth the new order was not yet here but just around the corner. And despite Jesus's own words, it had remained just around the corner for two millenia.

The almost insupportable sufferings that were to precede the establishment of God's kingdom were an inevitable consequence of living as if the kingdom had arrived when in truth it had not. Yet Jesus believed that these sufferings would hasten the kingdom. This belief was again part of his Jewish inheritance, derived in large part from the writings of the prophet Isaiah, who in Chapter 53 of his book had described the unique role of the suffering servant of God. In this conviction, Jesus went to his death. Similarly, his followers must be prepared to suffer to speed the coming of the kingdom. No one was allowed to await it passively.

In addition, the idea that the disciples must keep secret their insights into the imminent future meant that, in this world, they were apparent fools for so suffering. Schweitzer held that the messianic status of Jesus was only a partially kept secret. The story of his transfiguration, Peter's confession that he was the Son of God, and the triumphant entry into Jerusalem all seemed, at least in the Gospel tradition, to be proclaiming him as the Messiah, albeit a Messiah whose destiny was to suffer.

What readers must instantly acknowledge is that, in these late writings, Schweitzer—accused as he had been of abandoning any belief in God, of mingling essential Christianity with a pantheistic love of world religions, and of willingly rejecting any part of holy scripture that did not accord with his own preconceived ideas—was brilliantly synthesizing the most subtle and difficult elements of the Christian biblical tradition into an almost irresistible ethical and mythological blend. The man who in his early years had been attacked as distorting the biblical evidence was in fact blending each element—however unsympathetic to modern thought—into a seductive unity.

But was this the Jesus of history or merely another example of a theologian painting a portrait of Jesus in his own image? Schweitzer lived through cataclysmic times, through what he recognized as a crisis of civilization. He suffered from these cataclysms. He also derived from his portrait of Jesus an ethical stance appropriate to living through them. If civilization was doomed, then acts of heroic service and sometimes suffering were the only appropriate responses for someone who would not abandon morality altogether.

Yet sometimes Schweitzer failed to note how the experience of such cataclysmic times also affected other men's and women's vision of Jesus. Schweitzer rejected the notion of Jesus as the patron saint of the bourgeoisie; but others too, seeing this, perceived Jesus as far more politically committed than even Schweitzer did. They saw Jesus as seeking to transform the contemporary world—and failing to do so. In their view he died not as a pacifist, but as a revolutionary. These features of Jesus the revolutionary play no part in Schweitzer's portrait of his master.

Schweitzer also failed to note two other developments in contemporary religious thinking. One was the revelation, particularly in the ancient Jewish texts discovered at Qumran, of the remarkable diversity in the eschatological ideas in Judaism around the time of Jesus. Schweitzer took the scholarly view of first-century Palestinian Jews, which prevailed in the first half of this century. It was, we now know, an inadequate view.

The second development was the development of a far more radical notion of the sources on which the Gospel writers drew. Scholars began to posit the existence of an oral tradition that predated them. In the preaching of Jesus's first followers, it was argued, his words and stories might often have been given a new setting, which would subtly alter their significance.

That said, Schweitzer's analysis of the quest of the historical Jesus remains one of the most entrancing and incisive works of intellectual history ever written. "Jesus of Nazareth," Schweitzer insisted, "will not allow himself to be modernized." Unfortunately, that is precisely what theologians and historians had attempted to do ever since they began to seek out the historical Jesus. "Not only did each epoch find its reflection in Jesus; each individual created him according to his own character."

Schweitzer's own *Quest of the Historical Jesus* in part set about displaying this process but also wished to strip the Christian Savior of the dogmatic garments in which he had been clothed. The book glitters with epigrams and startling insights. "There is no historical task which so reveals a man's true self as the writing of a life of Jesus," he declares, adding instantly, "No vital force comes into the figure unless a man breathes into it all the hate or the love of which he is capable."

The stronger the hate or the love, Schweitzer held, the more lifelike is the resulting portrait. "For hate as well as love can write a life of Jesus, and the greatest of them are written with hate." Hermann Samuel Reimarus hated the supernatural nimbus which surrounded Jesus and wished to strip it away. So did David Friedrich Strauss.

Reimarus wisely kept his opinions to himself, and his study of the aims of Jesus and his disciples was published only in 1778, ten years after the author's death. Not so Strauss. In 1835, as a young man of twenty-seven, he openly published his views. "His *Life of Jesus* was his ruin," observed Schweitzer. Yet he quotes what Strauss wrote twenty-five years later:

> I might well bear a grudge against my book, for it has done me much evil. [Schweitzer adds, "And rightly so!" the pious will exclaim.] It has excluded me from public teaching in which I took pleasure and for which I had perhaps some talent; it has torn me from natural relationships and driven me into unnatural ones; it has made my life a lonely one. And yet when I consider what it would have meant had I suppressed the doubts which were at work in my mind—then I bless the book which had doubtless done me grievous harm outwardly, but which preserved the inward health of my mind and heart, and, I doubt not, has done the same for many others also.

Schweitzer added, "Before him Bhardt had his career broken in consequence of revealing his beliefs about the life of Jesus; and after him Bruno Bauer."

Schweitzer' *Quest* begins with the work of Reimarus, who was born in 1694. Astonishingly, before Reimarus no one had attempted to form any historical conception of the life of Jesus. In spite of all Reimarus's shortcomings, Schweitzer judged that "his work is perhaps the most splendid achievement in the whole course of the historical investigation of the life of Jesus, for he was the first to grasp the fact that the world of thought in which Jesus moved was essentially eschatological."

If Schweitzer chose Reimarus as the first historian of his *Quest*, he insisted that the whole study fell into two periods: before and after Strauss. The dominant interest in the first period Schweitzer characterized as the question of miracle, of what terms are possible between an historical treatment and the acceptance of supernatural events. "With the advent of Strauss the problem found a solution, viz., that these events have no rightful place in the history, but are simply mythical elements in the sources." Meanwhile, two other central topics were emerging: the eschatological, perceived by Reimarus, and the problem of the self-consciousness of Jesus, first emphasized in a life of Jesus published by Karl August Hase in 1929.

Part of the power of Schweitzer's study derives from the fact that he hero-worshiped some of the theologians with whom he most disagreed. "In order to understand Strauss, one must love him," he begins one chapter. "He was not the greatest, and not the deepest of theologians, but he was the most absolutely sincere. His insight and his errors alike were the insight and errors of a prophet. And he suffered a prophet's fate." As for Bruno Bauer, Schweitzer, himself not yet thirty, observes that when he first began to investigate the gospel history he was just at the beginning of his twenties, "that critical age when pupils often surprise their teachers, when men begin to find themselves and show what they are, not merely what they have been taught."

Schweitzer's analyses drive his audience to read these long-dead theologians for themselves. As the eccentric Bauer became more radical, Schweitzer noted that his writing became biting, injurious to his opponents, and ill-tempered. "In spite of his hatred of the theologians, which is pathological in character, like his meaningless punctuation, his critical analyses are always exceedingly acute." Bauer, he remarks, like Reimarus, exercised both a terrifying and a disabling influence on New Testament studies, not least because Bauer went so far as to declare that there never was any historical Jesus. Schweitzer believed that there was, but he judged that Bauer's *Criticism of the Gospel History* was worth a good dozen lives of Jesus simply because, "As we are only now coming to recognise after half a century, his work is the ablest and most complete collection of the difficulties of writing the life of Jesus that is anywhere to be found."

Schweitzer himself could be as injurious and biting as Bauer when he fell upon historians whose work he despised. In 1863, *La Vie de Jésus*, by the Frenchman Ernest Renan, was almost the first to bring to the Catholic world the insights of German critical theology. The book brought about Renan's dismissal as professor of Semitic languages at the Collège de France. Yet Schweitzer found his work sentimental, artificial, and subjective "in the worst sense of the word." The Alsatian mocked the Frenchman's portraits of "the gentle Jesus, the beautiful Mary, and the fair Galileans who formed the retinue of the 'amiable carpenter'" as figures that "might have been taken over in a body from the shop-window of an ecclesiastical emporium in the Place Saint-Sulpice."

True, Schweitzer describes Renan's study as a literary masterpiece. But he reserves his greatest sarcasm for Renan's account of the death and resurrection of Jesus. No longer in the Place Saint-Sulpice, Renan seems to have found his way to the cemetery of Père Lachaise in describing an entombment which really took place in Palestine. Renan apostrophizes the dead Jesus as if commissioned to pronounce the final allocution over a member of the French Academy. "Rest now, amid thy glory, noble pioneer. Thou conqueror of death, take the scepter of thy kingdom, into which so many centuries of thy worshipers shall follow thee, by the highway which thou hast opened up."

For the resurrection, the scene shifts to a theatre, and the event happens (or maybe does not happen) so fast as to take the spectators by suprise: "The bell rings; the curtain begins to fall; the swing seats tilt. The epilogue is scarcely heard: 'Jesus will never have a rival. His religion will again and again renew itself; his story will call forth endless tears; his sufferings will soften the hearts of the best; every successive century will proclaim that among the sons of men there has not arisen a greater than Jesus.'"

When he treats the liberal lives of Jesus, Schweitzer chronicles what he dubs the struggle against eschatology. He charts the fashion in which any unpalatable source in the four Gospels was jettisoned by successive critics either as a later invention of the church, or else as a mistaken shaping of history by the Gospel writers themselves. Jesus increasingly was cast in the image of his late-nineteenth- and early-twentieth-century biographers. Schweitzer notes with heavy irony the 1905 attempt of Gustav Frenssen to write "a life of the Saviour portrayed according to German research as the basis for a spiritual rebirth of the German nation." He mocks the Christian socialist Albert Kalthoff not so much for holding that Jesus never existed as for painting his image in smudgy red ink on blotting paper. He notes that the vast number of uselessly imaginative lives of Jesus "shrink into remarkably small compass on close examination: when one knows two or three of them one knows them all." Paul de Régla, among these imaginative inventors of fiction, comes in for especial criticism. Schweitzer quotes him on the beauty of the infant Jesus. "His eyes were not exceptionally large, but were well-opened, and were shaded by long, silky, dark-brown eyelashes and rather deep-set. They were of a blue-grey colour, which changed with changing emotions, taking on various shades, especially blue and brownish-grey."

Brilliantly, the penultimate chapter of the book considers not only William Wrede's seminal work on the messianic secret in the Gospels but also Schweitzer's own *Secret of the Messiahship and the Passion*, both of which had been published in 1901 on the selfsame day. Both books, Schweitzer knew, cast doubt on virtually every contemporary theologian. Modern historical theology, he said, "warned that the dyke was letting in water, had sent a crowd of masons to repair the leak, ignorant of the fact that the whole masonry had been undermined and needed rebuilding from its foundation. Or, to vary the metaphor, theology has come home to find the broker's marks on all the furniture, and then continued as before quite comfortably, ignoring the fact that it will lose everything if it does not pay its debts."

Schweitzer quotes with approval Wrede's attack on other biblical critics. "It finally comes to this," Wrede wrote, "that each critic retains whatever portion of the traditional sayings of Jesus that can be fitted into his own construction of the facts and his own conception of historical probability, and rejects the rest." The result, in Schweitzer's own words, is a Jesus designed by rationalism, endowed with life by liberalism, and clothed in historical garb by modern theology.

Against this Schweitzer set a Jesus to whom the religion of the present cannot ascribe, according to the long-cherished custom, its own thoughts and ideas. In its quest of the historical Jesus, theology supposed that by loosing him from the bands earlier theologians had bound him with, they could bring Jesus directly into our own time as a savior and teacher. "But he does not stay," declared Schweitzer. "He passes by our time and returns to his own." And the theologians—because of their own integrity—have had to let him go. Their Jesus was too small, forced into conformity with their own human standards and a human psychology.

At the very end of his *Quest* Schweitzer's own passionate beliefs at this moment suddenly force themselves to the surface. In his view, the true historical Jesus had overthrown the modern Jesus, rising against the modern spirit and sending on earth not peace but a sword. "He was a teacher, not a casuist. He was an imperious ruler. Because he was so in his inmost being, he could think of himself as the Son of man." The Jesus Schweitzer proclaimed as significant for his own times was not the historical Jesus, "but the spirit which goes forth from him and in the spirits of men and women strives for new influence and rule, the spirit which overcomes the world."

So (to use the words of a French scholar, Etienne Trocmé), the Jesus of Schweitzer, like "the Jesus of his adversaries, became another chapter—however exceptional—in the history of ideas." Yet, however flawed, this vision of Jesus helps enormously to explain the man Schweitzer was and the missionary he became. In later years Schweitzer never abandoned the passionate importance that the young man of twenty had afforded to Matthew 10—a single chapter in the whole of the New Testament. It was as a passionate young man that he also determined to prove the truth of his convictions not simply by intellectual writings but by living them. Thirty was the age at which Jesus began his public ministry. Till the age of thirty Schweitzer felt free to devote himself to science and art. Thenceforth his life would be one of service to his fellow human beings.

In 1910 the book was brilliantly translated into English by the Cambridge theologian F. C. Burkitt, who astutely changed its title (from *Reimarus to Wrede*) to *The Quest of the Historical Jesus*. By now Albert Schweitzer discovered some of the obloquy that had befallen some of the theologians he himself had written about. The message of his *Quest of the Historical Jesus* proved far from welcome to many of his fellow Christians. Long-forgotten authorities attempted to debunk his book and reassure the traditionalists.

When the Church Congress of 1910 met at Cambridge, Dr. R. H. Charles was at hand to declare that "much of Schweitzer's structure was based on sand." For good measure, Dr. Charles added that, "It was also in many cases built with untempered mortar." Schweitzer's insistence that Jesus's teaching was primarily eschatological rather than ethical was "hopelessly wrong." Schweitzer's reconstruction of the life and teaching of Jesus was "wrong in most of its positions." Finally, Schweitzer was foolish to assume that the words attributed to Jesus in Matthew, Chapter 10, were actually addressed by him to his disciples.

Further reassurance was provided by the warden of Keble College, Oxford, who said that although a great deal of Jesus's language was the language of crisis, it was perfectly consistent with his belief that after the crisis was over there would be a great development of human life along ethical and moral lines. And the dean of St. Patrick's, Dr. J. H. Bernard, roundly declared that "unhappily Dr. Schweitzer's constructive theory was even further removed from the historical faith of Christendom than the liberalism which he deprecated."

The following year at the annual meeting of the Free Church Council in Portsmouth, Professor J. H. Moulton, so *The Times* reported, "dealt with the sensation caused by Schweitzer's theory of the historical Jesus, which Professor Burkitt had accepted and his colleague Professor Inge had condemned as blasphemous." The problem with the theory, said the professor, was the extent to which it made Jesus, in declaring that the kingdom of God was coming soon, the subject of an illusion. But, Moulton continued, "There is no need for fear. The foreshortening of history which made Jesus see the vivid future so near was the inevitable condition of the real humanity he had taken upon himself."

Such attacks, misguided though they were, soon presented Schweitzer with a major problem, simply because the missionary society which he hoped to serve was run almost entirely by traditionalists. In 1904 he had read an article in which Alfred Boegner, a fellow Alsatian and president of the Paris Evangelical Missionary Society to non-Christian People, had appealed for workers to serve its mission in French Equatorial Africa. The society, Boegner wrote, needed "men and women who can simply rely on the Master's call." On the eve of his thirtieth birthday, believing that he himself had heard the Master's words, "Follow me," as he read the article, Schweitzer suddenly felt that, "my search was over."

Schweitzer would soon bare his soul about missions in a sermon of January 6, 1905, preached in Saint-Nicolas, Strasbourg. "For me missionary work is essentially not a religious matter," he declared. "First and foremost it is a humane duty that our states and nations have never undertaken. Only the religious, the simple folk, have acted on it in the name of Jesus." He was scathing about the motives of politicians and national leaders as they gazed across the sea. They brooded merely on countries to be taken under their own protection—which meant to be annexed. They considered only what they might siphon out of those countries for their own advantage. "We are robber states," said Schweitzer. "Where are the workers, tradesmen, teachers, professors and doctors ready to go to these countries and there work to bring about the blessings of civilisation?" he asked. "This 'noble' culture of ours," he continued, "speaks so piously of human dignity and the rights of man and then disregards the dignity and rights of countless millions, treading them underfoot simply because they live overseas or because their skins are of a different colour or because they are unable to help themselves."

Only the missionaries, Schweitzer believed, had stepped into the breach and done their best for such people—regardless of whether or not they were succeeding in preaching their own gospel. Above all, missionary work was in his eyes "atonement for the crimes of violence done in the name of Christian nations." Native peoples had been robbed of their land and enslaved. "The scum of mankind has been let loose on them," he said. "Think of the atrocities that have been perpetrated on people subservient to us: how we have systematically ruined them with alcohol and all the rest of our 'gifts.'"

One of Schweitzer's early professors, Lucius, had first alerted him to this notion of atoning for the evil done by whites to the black races when he lectured in the mid-1890s one hot summer afternoon. Schweitzer now proclaimed, "We must make atonement for all the terrible crimes which we read of in the newspapers." He added, "We must also atone for still worse crimes which we do not read of in the newspapers, crimes shrouded in the silence of the jungle night."

With such convictions, he was galled to discover that some leading members of the Paris Evangelical Missionary Society happened to regard him as a heretic. Schweitzer determined to visit them one by one to convince them of his spiritual credentials, but Boegner dissuaded him. In the end, after much prevarication, the committee accepted Schweitzer—but on what seem, in retrospect, the absurdest conditions. One was that he should not preach his version of the Christian Gospel but simply serve as a medical missionary. The other was that he should entirely finance himself. Schweitzer declared that once he arrived in the Congo he would remain as mute as a carp. It was a promise he completely failed to keep. But for the rest of his life, his missionary work and his jungle hospitals were financed, often with great difficulty, entirely by his own efforts.

In the meantime, the theologian and musician needed to qualify as a doctor of medicine.

CHAPTER 6

◆

Teacher and Medical Student

A lbert Schweitzer's generosity was willful and often spontaneous. It invariably reflected his iron will. After taking his first degree in 1899, he was faced with an unexpected choice. His tutor, Theobald Ziegler, himself a former theologian, insisted that if Schweitzer wanted to go forward as a lecturer in philosophy, he would have to give up preaching sermons. The conflict between one who proclaimed and one who quested was, thought Ziegler, too stark.

A Tübingen publisher, alerted to Schweitzer's genius by Holtzmann, was in the process of publishing an expanded version (one which no doubt took into consideration Ziegler's belief that the style was heavy and monotonous, and that there were too many exaggerated recapitulations) of his thesis on the religious philosophy of Kant. A successful academic career as a philosopher seemed assured. But Schweitzer also needed his pulpit. "By now preaching was for me an inner necessity," he wrote. "I felt it as something wonderful to be allowed to speak to my assembled fellow men and women on the deepest questions of existence."

Later, he confessed that before leaving for Africa after his final sermon at Saint-Nicolas, Strasbourg, giving up preaching and lecturing in theology were such great sacrifices that he avoided as far as possible even passing the church and university because the very sight of the places where he had carried on work that he imagined he would never resume was too painful for him.

So he chose theology rather than philosophy. And he also chose to relinquish his scholarship, after enjoying its annual emolument for little more than a year. A fellow student named Jäger, who later ran the Protestant Gymnasium in Strasbourg, was desperate for money to continue his Semitic studies. Schweitzer, who had originally planned an excursion to England and perhaps even farther afield, gave up his plans, allowed his scholarship to pass into the pocket of Jäger, and set about finding new employment to enable him to take his next degree, for which he planned to write a thesis on the Last Supper.

Already Schweitzer was intending to make an ambitious mark on the theological world. "I had formed the plan of writing a history of the Last Supper in connection both with the life of Jesus and with the history of primitive Christianity." The subject was central to an understanding of the crucial moment in the origins of Christianity. Jesus, about to go to his death, celebrates in secret a last supper with his disciples and then apparently enjoins them to continue celebrating such ritualistic meals in remembrance of him. The church had continued to obey this command. In consequence, wrote Schweitzer, the Last Supper "stands at the central point at which the faith of Jesus develops into the faith of the primitive church."

Schweitzer's approach to his chosen subject was first of all to review the understanding of this crucial meal as displayed by nineteenth-century theologians. Second, he took a coolly rational look at the original New Testament texts that speak about this sacramental meal. This task not only gained him the degree of licentiate in theology but also helped to form the introduction to volume one of his book on the Last Supper, which J. B. Mohr of Tübingen published in 1901.

Next, Schweitzer intended to analyze what he called "the secret of Jesus's messiahship and passion," and this, as well as gaining him his next degree, underlay volume two of the book. But for the most part his thoughts on these subjects were for a time communicated only in his lectures. In the winter of 1902 and 1903 Schweitzer's pupils gathered together on Saturday mornings at ten for an hour-long lecture on the understanding of baptism and the Last Supper in the New Testament and the first two Christian centuries—lectures that were repeated in the winters of 1906 and 1907 and of 1909 and 1910.

He had been relieved of the problem of finding somewhere to live when his old university rooms in the Collegium Wilhelmitanum and the garden there, where he loved to meditate and study, were made available to him—by now, though, at a modest rent. In December, a new source of income became available when Schweitzer was appointed an assistant clergyman of the church of Saint-Nicolas, the same church his uncle, Albert Schillinger, had served some three decades previously. What is more, the two full-time pastors of the church had been, respectively, one of his father's predecessors at Gunsbach and an intimate friend of his mother's brother. Here was a warm welcome. Shortly he would submit to a modest examination and become their regular curate. Schweitzer almost fluffed this simple examination when he dismissed with evident sarcasm a hymn written by one of his examiners. Otherwise, he passed with ease.

The church of Saint-Nicolas paid him a hundred German marks a month, which was more than enough to cover his rent and pay for his daily bread. In return, Schweitzer ran the intimate afternoon services, taught the children's catechism classes during school terms, and taught some doctrine. Schweitzer recalled that one of the congregation complained to his superiors that his sermons were too short. Schweitzer's response was that he was no more than "a poor pastor who had to stop talking when he had nothing more to say."

The following year he could afford to go to Bayreuth again, seeking another meeting with Cosima Wagner, whom he had already met when she was receiving visitors at Heidelberg and who would later deign to call on him in Strasbourg. His visit was enlivened by a meeting with his Aunt Mathilde, the sister of his father's eldest brother. As their visit coincided with the season of the Oberammergau passion play, staged once every ten years, he and Aunt Mathilde set off together to attend a performance in the exquisite Bavarian village. Schweitzer admired the rustic simplicity of the performers, the magnificent mountain range that serves as a backdrop to the performance, and little else about the play. The text, though recently revised, was for him ridiculously stilted; he found the staging far too theatrical; and Rochus Dedler's music seemed to him simply banal.

A year later, on the death of the principal of the Theological College at Strasbourg, Schweitzer was asked to run the college for six months while the new principal, Gustav Anrich, was still at work as pastor of Lincolnsheim. Schweitzer was moving up the academic ladder. Anrich replaced him but stayed in his new job for only two years before moving on to become professor of church history at Tübingen. His successor was Schweitzer. Happily, the post carried a salary of two thousand marks a year. In October 1903, Schweitzer moved into the spacious principal's lodgings, rejoicing that since he still retained his curate's salary, he could also afford to retain his old rooms for his personal study.

Would the twenty-eight-year-old scholar and teacher have been entrusted with the oversight of theological students had his radical cast of mind been more widely known at the time of his appointment? If not, his students were fortunate in the timing of Schweitzer's years as principal. Tireless at study, ever ready to play for visitors on the grand piano in his lodgings, lecturing in Hebrew and New Testament Greek, running a biweekly course on both the Old and the New Testaments, Schweitzer remained always available to his students—to the extent that he even shared their dining room. In addition, he would spend the evenings and sometimes most of the night writing about Bach.

A year later Schweitzer made his decision to go to French Equatorial Africa. But his theological genius remained alive. In the middle of 1905 he decided to alert his students to the long story of the attempt to discover the historical Jesus, announcing a series of lectures on Wednesday and Friday afternoons devoted to this quest from the era of David Friedrich Strauss, the so-called heretic whom Schweitzer believed needed to be loved in order to be understood. One year later, the expanded version of these lectures was published as his *Quest of the Historical Jesus*, branding Schweitzer a heretic in the eyes of conservative scholars, not to speak of the committee of the Paris Evangelical Missionary Society.

The theologian, philosopher, and musician had by then enrolled as a medical student. "For years I had been expressing myself in words, following with joy the calling of a teacher of theology and a preacher," he explained. "But this new form of activity I represented to myself not as talking about the religion of love but as actually putting it into practice." He wanted to be a doctor, he said, "in order to work without having to talk"—though in truth he never ceased to teach, talk, and write for the rest of his long life. In the first months of this new life, he finished writing both his work on organ-building and the last chapter of his *Quest*.

Schweitzer once more made one of his quixotic financial sacrifices by resigning as principal of the theological college in the spring of 1906. Friedrich Curtius, the stepson of the classical scholar, offered him the use of his attic, and Schweitzer's former students helped him to carry his belongings there. Continually he brooded about the plight of the inhabitants of the African colonies. "I had read about the physical miseries of the natives in the virgin forests," he wrote. "I had heard about them from missionaries, and the more I thought about this the stranger it seemed to me that we Europeans troubled ourselves so little about the great humanitarian task which offers itself to us in far-off lands." Schweitzer the preacher meditated on Jesus's parable of the rich man and the beggar Lazarus. "We are Dives," he asserted, "for through the advances of medical science we know a great deal about disease and pain and possess innumerable means of fighting them." Out in the colonies sat wretched Lazarus, suffering even more from illness and pain and with absolutely no means of fighting them.

Schweitzer revealed another side to this decision in a letter to the music critic Gustav von Lüpke. "Am I supposed to devote my life to making ever fresh critical discoveries, so as to become a famous theologian, and to go on training pastors who will also sit at home?" he asked, answering, "It became clear to me that this is not my life. I want to be a simple human being, to do something small in the spirit of Jesus." Yet his letter was disingenuous, as was a remark he slipped into his book *On the Edge of the Primeval Forest:* "I gave up my position of professor in the university of Strasbourg, my literary work and my organ-playing in order to go as a doctor to French Equatorial Africa." Of these three supposed sacrifices, Schweitzer abandoned only his posts in the university. He never ceased to play the organ. He never gave up his literary work.

Nor, initially, did he give up his professorship. Theoretically, no one could be a member of two disciplines in the University of Strasbourg. The members of the faculty of medicine simply waived their rules and allowed Schweitzer to attend lectures, free of charge, as a colleague. Schweitzer abandoned preaching at Saint-Nicolas and lecturing to university students only in 1912, when he was obliged to move to Paris to qualify in tropical medicine.

But the work was hard, and Schweitzer's life now became, as he put it, "a continuous fight against fatigue." His heroic will kept him going. "Whenever I was inclined to feel that the years I should have to sacrifice were too long, I reminded myself that Hamilcar and Hannibal had prepared for their march on Rome by their slow and tedious conquest of Spain." His goddaughter, Suzi, was by now a perpetual resource for him whenever he retreated to Gunsbach—especially in view of the fact that his parents, especially his mother, had been mortified at the news that her splendid son was to abandon everything he had achieved and become a missionary. Another support was Adèle

Herrenschmidt, now in her midfifties, still ready to holiday with Schweitzer in the Alps.

It nonetheless remained a minor miracle that Schweitzer, ever ready to address the International Music Society on organ-building (as he did in Vienna in 1909) or to help with the restoration of the Silbermann organ at Saint-Thomas, Strasbourg, managed to qualify as a doctor, let alone as a specialist in tropical medicine. And even as a doctor, he remained a theologian. The thesis he wrote for his degree was devoted to the psychiatric study of the life of Jesus.

Part of the problem, which Schweitzer here addressed, had been created, as he confessed, by himself. "I myself was once reproached with presenting him as a visionary or even someone under the sway of delusions." Was a Jesus who harbored such errors about the imminent arrival of the kingdom of God truly sane? When Schweitzer began working on the thesis, which took a year to write, he had the nasty feeling that to submit such a personality as Jesus to a psychiatric analysis was deeply repugnant, save for one overriding consideration: that "reverence for truth must be exalted above everything else."

Schweitzer set out to collate and examine everything that had been published medically on the supposed mental derangement of Jesus. "My task was to decide, from the medical point of view, whether this peculiar messianic consciousness of his was in any way connected with some psychic disturbance." Schweitzer's conclusion was that none of the medical experts who considered Jesus insane was right, simply because not one of them had troubled to become sufficiently familiar with the historical side of the question." Being the man he was, Schweitzer made sure that his study was published.

Far less well known or noted was Schweitzer's contribution to the study of Saint Paul. Some scholars regarded this as his finest work, and others severely attacked it; yet it was Schweitzer's *Quest* that caught the public eye. For Schweitzer himself, to turn to the study of Paul was a logical extension of his work on Jesus. He announced a series of lectures on Paul's letter to the Galatians in 1906, the year of the publication of his *Quest*, delivering them in the summer term. He later confessed that the time spent preparing these lectures severely taxed the energy he was devoting to the study of medicine, begun the previous year. In 1908 he passed his probationary exam as a doctor and was now working voluntarily in a hospital. But he was becoming fascinated by a new facet of the Christian tradition: what he described as "the remarkable Pauline doctrine of being "in Christ" and dying and rising with him." There was a clear link with Schweitzer's earlier convictions, for he felt that there must be some eschatological explanation of this teaching.

So, in the midst of all his other toils, as he later recalled, "By night I spent much time attempting to finish my history of the technical exploration of the conceptual world of Paul." The result of these labors was published in 1911 and translated into English the following year under the title *Paul and His Interpreters: A Critical History*. Schweitzer himself never ceased to hold that most of these scholars had transformed Paul's thoughts into something quite incompatible with "the originality and the grandeur of the man who had revealed them."

He had put in a great deal of work. This particular history initially had been planned as a mere introduction to Schweitzer's book on Paul and as a companion to his *Quest of the Historical Jesus*. As with his study of the psychology of Jesus, Schweitzer was concerned with reconciling the complications and apparently contradictory elements in the teachings of Paul as set out by most contemporary and recent theologians. Planning this study as a short preliminary work before tackling the question of Paul's eschatology, Schweitzer's little work turned out to be so long that he was obliged to publish it as a book on its own.

The reaction of most scholars was biting. First, they detailed the extraordinary lacunae in the book: no mention, for example, of Schweitzer's fellow Strasbourg professor, Eduard Reuss, who had set forth a powerful appraisal of Paul in a volume that appeared in 1852; no mention of Franz Overbeck's even more seminal analysis of Christian theology in 1872, which insisted that the central characteristic of primitive Christianity was a passionate belief in the imminent return of Christ; and the complete omission of any consideration of influential Catholic theologians. (Schweitzer himself had only in part disarmed such criticism by pleading lack of English when it came to analyzing British theologians.)

Next, Schweitzer's critics observed that Schweitzer's obsession with eschatology led him to ignore completely other essential elements of Paul's thought: his teaching on justification by faith, for example, and his doctrine of sin. Schweitzer had insufficiently grappled with the profundity of the Pauline texts (whereas many of his critics had, of course, spent their lives writing uninspired, if immensely scholarly, commentaries on some of them). And this time around, few were willing to allow Schweitzer to play havoc with the reputations of his predecessors. "It simply will not do to take for more or less imbeciles almost all those who have worked before in the same domain," wrote J. Kögel.

Perhaps Schweitzer was led astray by his methodology. Such had been the success of his *Quest* that here again he set about a systematic account of all his predecessors in the field since the Reformation. But this time he was evidently bored with many of them, and the analysis of the early pedants is perfunctory and uninspired. His narrative only comes alive when he starts to assess the work of the nineteenth-century scholar Bruno Bauer—even though he considered Bauer's conclusions entirely negative.

Indeed, only two scholars receive any real praise throughout the book. The first, Hermann Lüdemann, had published a work on Paul in 1872 that carefully distinguished two "anthropologies" in the apostle's teachings. The first was Jewish, with its concern for a physical salvation. The second was Hellenic, with its insistence on a spiritual salvation. Although Lüdemann preferred the Hellenic notion (which Schweitzer did not), insisting that Paul increasingly rejected his Jewish background, Schweitzer praised Lüdemann's "brilliant work." For, with many of his fellow scholars, Schweitzer was forced to grapple with the problem of explaining how Paul's version of Christianity, which seemed to him essentially Jewish, was so speedily transformed into a philosophy far more akin to contemporary Hellenism. "How could the exclusively Jewish and eschatological point of departure have evolved into the Greek understanding of the Gospel?" Lüdemann had cleared the decks for the task.

Schweitzer's second praiseworthy scholar was Richard Kabisch, who had written about the eschatology of Paul in 1893, "clearly setting out for the first time," in Schweitzer's view, "the great paradoxes which one finds in Paulinist eschatology." Wholly and deliberately, Kabisch insisted, Paul had rejected this world. For Paul, Christianity was already involved in the last things. "The morality he preaches and the religion he proclaims," Kabisch insisted, "are supremely the way by which we can enter that future glory."

Schweitzer's history of Pauline studies was then forgotten. Few Pauline scholars referred to it in their own subsequent works. For Schweitzer himself, the inevitable pain of these rebukes must have helped to make his next book on Paul the far more scholarly, well-expressed, and scrupulously researched volume that it turned out to be.

For the time being, the demands of his complex personality and incessant toil interrupted the work. Between 1911 and 1921 Schweitzer completed his medical qualifications, revised the second edition of his *Quest*, set to work on an edition of Bach's organ works, departed for Africa, was interned and fell ill, returned to Africa, and tirelessly gave concerts and raised money for the jungle hospital.

Surprisingly, then, in 1921 he was lecturing on Paul in London. When he set off again for Africa in 1924, in his luggage was a manuscript devoted to the mysticism of Paul the Apostle. He might almost as well have left it behind. So preoccupied was Schweitzer with the daily concerns of the hospital that the manuscript lay virtually untouched until he was ready to return to Europe in 1927.

At last Schweitzer determined to finish the study, devoting

every moment of spare time to Saint Paul. He wrote the final chapter in 1929 on board ship, on his return from Europe to French Equatorial Africa. His *Mysticism of Paul the Apostle* was published a year later. Schweitzer had by then become famous. The hostile public reactions which had greeted his *Quest of the Historical Jesus* failed to emerge this time, even though Schweitzer's assessment of Paul was more partial and less well-pondered than his assessment of Jesus.

Whereas his *Quest* went through six editions in his own life-time and was even reprinted as a pocket book paperback, Schweitzer's book on the mysticism of Saint Paul was reprinted only once. In consequence, it became an accepted part of the scholarly repository of specialists but never impinged in a major way, as the *Quest* did, on the consciousness of the general public. And whereas his fascination for Jesus and for J. S. Bach is evident throughout the years of his early manhood, neither in his writings, his preaching, or his Strasbourg lectures does Paul make the remotest impact until Schweitzer's thirty-first year. We simply possess a 1901 statement, in his treatise on the Last Supper, that Paul and Jesus both must have accepted the current eschatological views of their fellow Jews. His introduction to *The Mysticism of Paul the Apostle* adds that his studies turned upon two questions: "First whether alongside the eschatological inter-pretation of the preaching of Jesus there was room for another; and secondly what had happened to the original entirely escha-tological belief of the first Christians as Hellenistic ideas replaced it."

This was the logic behind Schweitzer's decision, having fin-ished his *Quest* and in the light of its conclusions, to go on to consider the teachings of Paul. Since with Jesus's death the king-dom of God had not been inaugurated, Paul was the chief of subsequent Christians who, so to speak, had to pick up the pieces. However faithful a Christian might wish to be to the founder, the faith needed some reinterpretation. Sharing Jesus's eschatological background, Paul nonetheless had to pour Chris-tianity into a different mold. Schweitzer speculated that he was possibly enabled to transform Jesus's eschatology partly because he selected different Jewish writings from those favored by Jesus on which to base his own beliefs. Paul preferred the books of Esdras and Baruch to Jesus's favored Enoch and Daniel.

Paul's genius also enabled him to incorporate belief in the death and resurrection of Jesus into his new conception of the last things. True, the Crucifixion had not brought about the coming of the kingdom. But Christ had risen from death. Christians today, Paul taught, could mystically share in the powers of that resurrection before rising again when the kingdom finally did arrive. The word *mystically* was crucial. Only thus could earthbound Christians share the first resurrection. The powers of the supernatural were now at work, transforming the visible world in accordance with the demands of the world to come.

The merits of Schweitzer's study of Paul lie in its author's incisiveness. He had the gift of asking directly the most simple questions and setting clearly against each other irreconcilable answers, forcing his readers (and himself) to a personal stance. "Either Jesus thought eschatologically," he wrote in his 1901 sketch of his Master's life, "or else he did not. He could not think eschatologically and non-eschatologically at the same time." So Schweitzer—to the great annoyance of his teacher Holtzmann, chose the option that had been set out by Johannes Weiss: that Jesus's message was solely eschatological. And so, he now declared, was Paul's.

His chief adversary was his former teacher Heinrich Julius Holtzmann. Holtzmann's magisterial study of New Testament theology, published in 1897, was (Schweitzer argued in the central chapter of his book) fundamentally flawed. Holtzmann's chief error, Schweitzer asserted, was to transform Paul's objective beliefs into subjective notions. In addition, Schweitzer asserted that Holtzmann erroneously taught that in Paul's mind Greek and Jewish elements lay in contradiction. That notion, said Schweitzer, enabled his teacher to avoid explaining Paul at all.

In contrast, Schweitzer utterly rejected the idea that Paul's theology was in any way influenced by Hellenistic ideas, even by the ideas of the Hellenistic Jews of his day. "Theological scholarship has been dominated by the desire to minimize as much as possible the element of Jewish apocalyptic in Jesus and Paul," he wrote. Instead, he said, "We must risk the 'one-sidedness' of trying to understand the doctrine of the apostle of the Gentiles entirely on the basis of primitive Jewish Christianity."

What Paul was attempting, Schweitzer believed, was to express his Jewish eschatology in Greek terms. This alone explained the numerous religious expressions he borrowed from contemporary Greek thought. In borrowing the expressions, he had not taken on board their pagan significance. Paul, Schweitzer asserted, understood salvation as "a cosmic event, which transforms the state of creation and inaugurates a new era for the world." But, he went on, there was a mystical element in this physical one. Paul seems to have supposed that by baptism the powers of this future transformation were already inserted, so to speak, in a Christian.

Schweitzer's high estimate of the importance of Paul shines throughout the book. First, he asserts that Paul is the sole person in primitive Christianity whom we really know—and we know him remarkably well. Next, Paul established once and for all the rights of thought, of speculation, in Christendom. Third, by insisting that where the spirit of Jesus reigns, there is freedom, Paul laid enormous importance on the quest for truth.

Fourth, as Schweitzer baldly put it, "Paul is a mystic." True, Schweitzer had his own notion of mysticism as something not irrational but, as he expressed it in this book, the common intellectual possession of all humanity. "This mysticism manifests itself whenever our thinking makes the supreme effort to understand the relationship of our personality to the universal," he wrote. At such moments the conscious personality rises above the illusive sensory belief that in our present lives we are in bondage to the earthly and the temporal. Distinguishing between appearance and reality, it catches sight of the eternal in what is transient; it distinguishes between appearance and reality; it recognizes the unity of all things in God; and it passes beyond the flux of becoming and distintegration into the peace of timeless being.

In an attempt to expound this fusion of time and eternity,

Schweitzer compared mystical insight into the world and eternity with a Bach fugue, which, though belonging to the eighteenth century, witnesses to a timeless musical truth. So, said Schweitzer, Christian mysticism throughout the centuries finds its timeless prototype in the mysticism of Paul the Apostle, in spite of the fact that Paul was bound by the limits of his own time.

Paul's specific contributions to Christian mysticism, averred Schweitzer, include the fact that he was the first Christian thinker to preach what Schweitzer dubbed "Christ-mysticism" rather than "God-mysticism." And he sowed the seeds for a crucial future development of Christianity: its absorption of Greek ideas and modes of thought. "Paul was not the one who introduced Greek modes of thought into early Christianity," Schweitzer argued, "but in his eschatological mysticism of being 'in Christ' he provided a setting in which Hellenization could grow."

In this book Schweitzer took care to put into the text far more of his own admiration of Paul than he had done in his history of Pauline scholarship. Paul, Schweitzer asserted, had "carried the primitive Christian faith to a pinnacle of achievement." Taking men and women along the path to salvation, he had delivered them to Christ. Some of this admiration was undoubtedly tendentious. In attempting to begin the central work of his life, Schweitzer himself had suffered at the hands of blinkered churchmen. So, in 1930, Paul seemed to him to reap praise as the "first Christian thinker to rebel against the authority of the church."

Yet the suspicion recurs that Schweitzer this time escaped criticism only because his personal stature was now of a different order. Once again the lacunae in his researches and references were staggering. A contemporary school of theologians was debating the problem of whether pre-Pauline sources had been inserted into the Pauline records. Schweitzer utterly ignored their writings. From the point of view of technical theologians, this curt way with parallel approaches to the Pauline texts severely vitiated some of Schweitzer's methodology. He would quote as genuinely Pauline words passages such as Romans 3:24–25 that other scholars increasingly were accepting as elements taken by Paul from earlier Christian traditions. And though (in spite of the detailed researches of his fellow scholars) Schweitzer still declared himself entirely opposed to the school of thought that saw Paul as a hellenizer, among those who would have disagreed with him was no less a person than the author of the Acts of the Apostles, who, in Chapter 17, portrays Paul at Athens proclaiming that the "unknown God" worshipped by some Greeks was the God of the Christians. Faced with such a text, Schweitzer roundly declared it unhistorical, arguing that Stoic pantheism was simply "inaccessible both to Judaism and to primitive Christianity."

As Schweitzer wrote in 1930, "A Christianity which dares not place historical truth at the service of spiritual truth displays no inner health, even if it is filled with faith." Nevertheless, his own contentions in *The Mysticism of Paul the Apostle* were set forward with a pugnacious alacrity that scarcely ever paused to allow him to argue his case with rigor. Scarcely ever offering learned footnotes, rarely referring to other scholars when setting out his own views, Schweitzer proceeded intuitively to offer a vision of Paul that not only was enticing but also eminently problematic.

Yet his work was now universally acclaimed. Even the brilliant Marburg professor Rudolf Bultmann, whose own Pauline researches had been completely passed over in Schweitzer's volume, described the conception of the book as truly grandiose. Another brilliant scholar, Martin Dibelius, acknowledged that Schweitzer had posed the decisive questions in the question of Saint Paul's beliefs. Maurice Goguel declared that Schweitzer had marvelously expounded the spirit of Paulinism. These judgments, typical of many, are as much a tribute to Schweitzer's increasing personal stature as the saint of Lambaréné as a testimony to his scholarship. And though his new book was as polemical as his previous Pauline study, no one this time around admonished him.

How, then, can one explain the appeal of a book which was

in so many respects swimming against the strong currents of contemporary theology? In one sense Schweitzer was offering a way out of the impasse he had presented to the Christian West in his *Quest*. By transforming the eschatology of Jesus into mysticism, his Paul enabled later generations of Christians to cope with the fact that the imminent coming of the kingdom of God had not happened. Jewish and early Christian eschatology made no sense to men and women of the 1930s; the notions of living "in Christ" and of being infused with his spirit might still inspire.

Yet Schweitzer seemed not to have utterly abandoned primitive eschatology. Positively, he was advancing the theses that Paul's idea of life "in Christ" took Jesus's own messianic eschatology to the utter limits. Jesus had bidden his followers, the "elect," to partake in his messianic mission, particularly by suffering as he did. For Paul, these messianic men and women were participating in eternal life, even before the coming of the kingdom of God.

Their new status transformed the Old World. The Jewish law no longer applied to them. Henceforth, for instance, no food was to be considered "unclean." The relations of the sexes were now to be seen in the light of eternal life (and here Paul counseled— though did not decree—that sexual congress between Christians should end). So were the relations between races, for the differences between Greeks and Jews, as well as those between male and female, were obliterated when all lived "in Christ." Thus Paul preached a new Christian liberation—and Schweitzer eagerly embraced it.

How then was exhibited the reality of death and resurrection with Jesus as proclaimed in the mysticism of Paul? Schweitzer replied that a person who suffered for his faith was dying in Christ. And those who were risen with Christ revealed this by their suffusion with his Holy Spirit. Here Schweitzer could appeal both to Paul's repeated affirmations of his own tribulations and also to the note of joy which is equally unmistakable in his writings.

One more point: However much suffering was essential in

Paul's understanding of Christianity, it was an ever recurring note in Schweitzer's attempt to come to terms with his own personal life. This clearly emerges in his preaching before World War I. In the pulpit of Saint-Nicolas, Strasbourg, on February 23, 1902, he took as his text Jesus's statement, recorded in the Fourth Gospel, that lifted up (on his cross), he would draw all men to him. For Schweitzer, this meant that he would draw all mankind to suffer with him. "The Lord will draw us after him into suffering." Paul the Apostle, Schweitzer continued, "speaks of himself in a time of great tribulation as filling up that which is lacking in the sufferings of Jesus. A beautiful saying. We too must all pass through suffering. We must not tremble or ask questions. We must know that misfortune is part of what is means to be a Christian."

The following May he was urging his congregation to take active steps to embrace such sufferings. "A man who does not act goes no further than the maxim, life means suffering and tribulation." A maxim is not enough, Schweitzer pronounced; the followers of Jesus will know that his strength can overcome any harm only when they experience pain and sorrow in their own lives—for initially Jesus brought to men and women not peace but a sword. Soon Schweitzer himself, along with his bride-to-be, would suffer far more than either of them had bargained for.

CHAPTER 7

❖

Africa and
Respect for Life

O nce qualified as a medical man, Schweitzer pointedly
insulted the committee members of the Paris Evangelical
Missionary Society by writing to say that since Jesus had
observed, "He that is not against me is for me," even a Muslim
ought to be acceptable to them if he wished to treat the sufferings of the natives. The committee had agreed to offer him a
house and a hospital in the Congo; the rest he would pay for
himself. By now he had already set about raising funds for his
project from his rich friends in Paris and Strasbourg. He gave an
organ recital in Paris to the same end, followed by a second one
at Le Havre. Pastors he had taught dunned cash out of their
parishes.

When sufficient money had been raised for the medical missionary and his nurse to live in Africa for at least a year and
Schweitzer had bought enough equipment for their first trip, he
was summoned to be grilled by the committee of the missionary
society. He refused, agreeing only to meet them one by one.
Schweitzer needed to beg a plot of land from the society, and so
it was at these meetings that the missionary doctor promised to

remain "as dumb as a carp" when he reached Africa—a promise he had no intention of keeping.

He also decided that his nurse ought to become his wife, or perhaps he felt obliged to marry her simply because few people, and particularly not her father, were pleased at the thought of an unmarried young woman leaving with her powerful male friend for the African jungle. So in January 1912, Schweitzer brought Hélène Bresslau to call on his family in Gunsbach, as a member of the Strasbourg cycling club.

She and Schweitzer had known each other for a dozen years. Hélène Bresslau's father, Harry, was a distinguished professor of medieval history at Strasbourg who had converted to Christianity from Judaism. A founding editor of the *Monumenta Germaniae historica*, this extremely learned man was also president of the Strasbourg Scientific Society and editor of the registers of the bishop of Strasbourg.

His daughter had studied art and music with the intention of becoming a teacher. After working as a governess in England and Russia, she became increasingly interested in social problems and in 1905 was apponted an assistant social worker and then inspector of orphanages for the Social Service Department of Strasbourg. Her superior described her as devoted to the work, extremely cultivated, and with a fine intelligence, as well as discreet and irreproachable. A report by the mayor of Strasbourg in 1905 noted that she possessed remarkable tact and was able to overcome the understandable resistance of parents who resented the intrusions of the Office of Social Work into their lives.

She was also an innovative radical. In 1907 she had taken an active part in setting up a home in Strasbourg-Heudorf to welcome unmarried mothers emerging from hospital. Her ally in this work was a woman named Elly Knapp, whose marriage ceremony to the future West German chancellor Theodor Heuss Albert Schweitzer had performed, smelling powerfully of disinfectant since he had just come from the operating theatre.

In short, the zeal and drive of Hélène Bresslau were almost the equal of Schweitzer's. Nor was she afraid of his intellect or rudeness. On the contrary, she would chide him for his rough Alsatian accent. Soon she was correcting the proofs of his books, even daring to improve the language of the ones in German. On Sundays she played the organ of Saint-Nicolas for his children's services. For a time, until Schweitzer resolved to work as a missionary, she even persuaded him that a suitable vocation, once he had reached the age of thirty, would have been to work with orphans himself. When this project fell through, she trained for a year and a half in hospitals in Frankfurt am Main and Stettin in order to qualify as a nurse and work in his projected jungle hospital.

Photographed in 1912 when she was in her midthirties, though severely dressed in her nurse's uniform she appears as a strikingly beautiful woman. On Hélène Bresslau's arrival at Gunsbach, Suzanne Oswald noted how fine and cultivated she was, adding later that "her frail body was inhabited by iron energy, and she was possessed of a steely will to work at Schweitzer's side in fulfillment of their mutual ideals." Suzanne remembered her wide gray eyes and rich brown hair. This splendid woman also adored to ski. It was a pursuit that cost her dearly, for in 1912 she went out on the slopes with Albert Schweitzer's brother Paul when the snow was thawing and Albert had begged her to stay indoors. Hélène fell badly and was left with a permanently disabled back.

The Gunsbach children, according to Suzanne, initially called Hélène Bresslau Auntie Respectable. But when Uncle Bery took the young Suzi in his arms, she was more than ready to accept her new aunt. The wedding took place in June 1912, first at a civil ceremony in Strasbourg on the fifteenth, with Harry Bresslau and Schweitzer's brother-in-law Albert Woytt (then a pastor at Oberhausbergen) as witnesses. Three days later, when the huge peonies in the garden of Schweitzer's mother were blooming, the religious wedding took place in Gunsbach.

From then until the pair set off for Africa, Schweitzer's young niece Suzanne recalled that she felt herself in heaven, for Albert and his new wife lived in the Gunsbach clergy house. She also remembered that her own family, with their sarcastic Alsace ways, scarcely made life easy for this woman from the other side of the Rhine. Albert too joined in the mockery, so that when Hélène lamented the slow workings of the German postal service, he mockingly observed that she forgot how her countrymen were busy building a massive navy and could have little time for anything else.

On other members of the household the imminent departure for French Equatorial Africa cast a darker shadow. In particular, Schweitzer's mother remained implacably opposed to the whole notion. Charles-Marie Widor, who also visited Gunsbach (traveling fourth class for the last part of the journey, out of deference to his distinguished pupil and collaborator) also tried to dissuade Schweitzer. Why, he asked, should a general go into the firing line with a rifle? Marcel Dupré recalled Widor telling the story: "Filled with deference, his head bowed, Schweitzer answered each argument with the words, 'Yes, master, but God calls me.' The next day Dupré asked Widor if he had managed to persuade Schweitzer not to renounce everything for this quixotic ambition. Widor replied, 'My poor Dupré, what do you say when a man tells you "God calls me"?' "

Though superficially a worldly wise dandy, Widor had seen deeper into Schweitzer's mind than many a contemporary and obviously recognized his dissatisfaction with the civilization of the West. Reading Søren Kierkegaard in 1905, Schweitzer had wondered whether Europe could ever recover from what he described as "spiritual decadence." Even earlier, in his Paris days, he had felt that there was a turn-of-the-century fatigue in the spirit of the times. "Had earlier hopes for the future of mankind been so high-pitched that men and women were finding it necessary to abandon them, limiting themselves to working only for the attainable?" he asked. For himself this would never do. "With the spirit of the age I am in complete disagreement," he wrote. For him, as he told Jean-Paul Sartre, "the essence of Christianity is the affirmation of a world which has gone through a period of world-negation." Paradoxically, to affirm the world, he needed to turn his back—at least temporarily—on the achievements of a society in which he had moved with such distinction.

But Schweitzer, though a headstrong visionary, was no fool. First, he registered at Gunsbach town hall a precautionary lifetime's lease on land overlooking Gunsbach, so keeping at least a a foothold in his homeland. Next, in spite of his determination—should his health hold out—to remain a missionary for the rest of his life, he wrote to the Protestant theology faculty at Strasbourg, asking, before he finally quit the university, for a two-year leave of absence in case some accident prevented his staying any longer in the northern Congo.

This time the faculty could not bend the rules. Such a sabbatical could be granted only if its purpose was connected with its own activities. Even so, the members insisted that Schweitzer keep the title "Professor," and added that should anything prevent his even leaving for Africa, he should instantly return to work among them.

If Hélène proved to be permanently disabled after her skiing accident, for the moment her husband's own exhaustion offered a respite of some six months before their departure. As a student doctor, his examiners invariably reported, whether of his dissection or his vivas, "very good." The problems of general and pathological anatomy, surgery, gynecology, obstetrics, ophthalmics, hygiene, and psychiatry all were successfully mastered. In February 1913, at the age of thirty-eight, he finally graduated as an expert in tropical medicine.

The day of his and Hélène's departure inexorably drew near. They had decided to leave on Good Friday. On March 9 he preached his farewell sermon in the church of Saint-Nicolas, Strasbourg. His text was "The peace of God, which passes all understanding, shall keep your hearts and minds in Christ Jesus." The imagery of this sermon speaks of seeing the world only distantly, as if Schweitzer were already envisaging Africa. "The peace of God is like the distant snow-covered peaks of mountains, which gleam in the sun as they rise above the mist." Below them, however, hidden in this mist, were foothills which everyone who would reach the peaks must climb. Many people, he declared, had grown content with living at a far lower level than this. They had never known the yearning for something greater, or if they had, they had lost that yearning. "They have arrived at the point where they say, 'The life I am leading now is all I desire. I shall arrange it to suit myself. I know my aim and I am satisfied with it.'" So they become content with what Schweitzer called "the trivialities of commonplace concerns."

If the morning of Good Friday 1913 dawned bright and sunny at Gunsbach, Suzanne Oswald remembered that the atmosphere in the pastor's home was heavy and dark. Albert asked his mother for his regular breakfast *Kugelhopf*. For a moment she sat like a statue at the table before speeding tight-lipped from the room. "That was hard for her son," wrote Suzi, "but he knew what he had to do." Then they were at the railway station. The train for Strasbourg came in slowly along the tracks, as if (again Suzi remarked) allowing the family sufficient time at the leavetaking to express its love and to wish the departing couple well. Schweitzer's mother alone remained unbending. Then Albert and Hélène climbed up into the last carriage, so as to be able to look back on their former home. After the train had pulled out of the station, no one spoke on the way back to the parsonage.

Schweitzer had told his congregation at Strasbourg on March 9, "As I prepare to leave you I know we shall not meet again for a long time." He was never to see his mother again.

After spending a night in Strasbourg, the couple took the train to Paris, so that the following day they could enjoy Charles-Marie Widor's Easter performance on the organ of Saint-Sulpice. The same afternoon they took another train for Bordeaux. Their luggage had gone before them. A significant indication that Schweitzer's intellectual activities were by no means finished was the fact that packed alongside the crockery for their hospital were enough books for the scholar to continue working on his projected book, *We Epigones*.

With considerable difficulty Schweitzer cleared their luggage through customs, and he and Hélène were able to board their final train to Pauillac and embark on the steamer *Europe*. Their journey proved stormy and uncomfortable. As Schweitzer found his own luggage smashing about the tossing cabin, he took comfort from the fact that the sound of smashing crockery could also be heard from the ship's galley and dining room.

Old Africa hands now advised the would-be missionaries on tricks of the trade. In the tropics, solar topees were vital (or so they were told), even if the day seemed cool. When the *Europe* called in at Dakar, Albert was so incensed to see two Africans ill-treating a horse that he physically pulled them off their over-loaded cart—an example of unconscious paternalism perhaps, or maybe simply the same care for animals that he had already dis-played as a young man.

When they reached the capital city of French Equatorial Africa the Schweitzers, by prearrangement, were welcomed by an American missionary. He introduced them to some members of his black congregation, whom Schweitzer favorably judged (on what grounds it is hard to conjecture, since he hardly knew them) as "free and modest." The *Europe* took them a few knots further on to Cap Lopez, where some of their luggage was trans-ferred to the paddle steamer *Alémbé*, and they set off up the Ogowe River on the final leg of their journey. Most of their lug-gage had to be left behind, to follow when the paddle steamer next sailed up the Ogowe.

As the *Alémbé* steamed up the Ogowe, the Schweitzers exult-ed in the wide fields of papyrus on either side, the bushes as tall as a man, the clumps of palm trees, the roots and brightly flow-ering creepers intruding into the river so that its banks were barely visible, and the rotting stems of once gigantic trees set amid the luxuriant greenery. He reveled in the birds, a heavily flying heron, a pair of ospreys circling in the sky, white and blue birds skimming the water. "Then—yes, they are unmistakable—from the branch of a palm tree hang a couple of swinging mon-key tails. Now we can see their owners. We are really in Africa!" Albert wrote.

The *Alémbé* stopped to fill up with wood at a little African village. The captain abused the village elder for not having enough logs, and they haggled about how the villagers should be paid. Eventually, the captain agreed to hand over liquor instead of cash—a practice that Schweitzer came increasingly to deplore. On this occasion, a trader standing next to him remarked that fifteen years earlier, when he first arrived in this part of Africa, such villages were flourishing spots. Alcohol had ruined them. Then the *Alémbé* sailed on, passing the place known as "Let's try," or Lambaréné, in the local dialect. Here Albert Schweitzer would build his most famous hospital, but in 1913 he and his wife sailed on to be met by two American missionaries whose station, further on at Andende, had been established in 1872 by American Presbyterians before being handed over to the Paris Evangelical Missionary Society.

Albert and Hélène were brought from the paddle steamer to the station in dugout canoes, welcomed, and shown to their wooden bungalow with its shaded veranda. Sitting on a packing case, they listened to the children singing their evening hymn. Darkness fell suddenly. Twelve hours later, at six o'clock in the morning, the sun rose with equal speed, the children sang their morning hymn, and the Schweitzers began work. They had not planned such a precipitous start. Save for a few drugs in Albert's trunk, their medical equipment was still on its way.

A fortnight passed before the paddle steamer brought the rest of the Schweitzers' luggage. To reach the shore, the special piano given to him by the Paris Bach Society needed a huge canoe of its own. By now, Albert and Hélène had fixed on the sole building that could be converted into a hospital: a filthy, leaking hut, till recently used as a hen coop. Whitewashing the dirty walls, Albert fixed up some shelves and put in an old camp bed. There was little room for storing medicine, so the Schweitzers had to give up part of their bungalow for this.

So far Schweitzer's agreement with the Paris Evangelical Missionary Society was scrupulously respected. The society had provided him with a free home and a hospital building. For his part, he offered medical services to the staff of the Congo mission and entirely paid for his own medical work. While he slowly built up the trust of the Africans, Schweitzer speedily charmed his fellow missionaries. The latent hostility of the committee of the missionary society to this supposed heretic was not shared by those working far out in the field. Preaching a simple message of Christian ethics to their black congregations, they insisted that Schweitzer's talents as a preacher should be added to theirs. So he ceased to be dumb as a carp.

Schweitzer soon perceived that his operating theatre in a former hen coop was inadequate. At their July conference held at Samkita, some fifty kilometers up the river, his fellow missionaries, who had to agree to any alteration in the original arrangements, readily accepted his request to build a new hospital according to his own design. What is more, they offered him four thousand francs toward the cost of building it. He created an extraordinary building, as brilliant a construction in its way as any of his theological speculations. Remarkably practical, it was oriented along the equator, so that the stifling sun never penetrated its wards. At each end corrugated-iron side walls supported a roof of calico, which defended the patients against mosquitoes. The other two walls were simply mosquito nets, though when storms raged they could be protected by wooden shutters.

Hélène and Albert desperately needed assistance, and help arrived in the form of a French-speaking African named Joseph Azowani. A skilled cook, Joseph first came to the hospital as a patient, but Albert Schweitzer was so struck with his intelligence that he invited him to stay as his interpreter and medical assistant. Joseph agreed and became the doctor's aid for half a century. Soon, from 8:30 each morning, the Alsatian doctor, aided by his wife, operated on patients beside the river Ogowe while Joseph sterilized the doctor's instruments by plunging them into boiling water. Hélène put the patients to sleep with anesthetics. Joseph pulled on his rubber gloves and came into the operating theatre.

Outide, the friends and relatives of patients sat or squatted, feeding themselves and obliged, if necessary, to feed their sick. Where they could, Schweitzer also obliged them to pay something toward the cost of treatment in the form of fruit or vegetables. Each morning, in both the Galoa and the Pahouin dialect, his six commandments were read out:

1) Spitting is strictly prohibited near the doctor's house.
2) Those who are waiting outside must not talk to each other loudly.
3) Patients and their friends are obliged to bring with them enough food for one day, since not everyone can be treated early.
4) Any person spending the night here without the doctor's permission will be sent away without any medicine.
5) All the bottles and tin boxes in which the medicines are dispensed must be returned.
6) In the middle of the month, when the paddle steamer has gone upstream, only urgent cases can be seen until the steamer sails down again, for the doctor is then writing to Europe to obtain more of his valuable medicines.

After each commandment, the listeners were expected to nod, to show that they understood and agreed. The harangue ended with a plea that the hearers spread the doctor's words throughout the neighboring villages.

Schweitzer had endless problems persuading patients not to take their medicines all at once. Some of his recuperating patients would bathe, unwisely, in the filthy Ogowe. Others inserted grubby fingers under their dressings to feel their wounds. Sometimes relatives crept inside his hospital and climbed into the patients' beds, forcing the sick to sleep on the floor. To stop their sores discharging, many patients resorted to the jungle remedy of covering the wound with powder made from the bark of a tree, which only made matters worse.

"Yet what do all these disagreeable problems count besides the joy of being here and working and helping?" Schweitzer wrote. Continually anxious about his supply of medicines, he declared that, "however limited one's means, how much one can do with them!" Looking back over two and a half months, he could say only that a doctor was terribly needed in Andende. "From a huge surrounding distance the natives avail themselves of his help, and with comparatively small means he can accomplish a quite disproportionate amount of good." A few days earlier a young African had told him, "Among us everyone is ill," and an old chief remarked, "Our country devours its own children."

By the end of their first nine months at Andende, Schweitzer and his wife had treated some two thousand patients. Their patients' chief complaints were skin diseases, malaria, sleeping sickness, elephantiasis, heart problems, leprosy, osteomyelitis, tropical dysentery, and hernias. Hernia operations were the ones Schweitzer had to perform most. As he observed, "Let not the sun go down upon your strangulated hernia" was a maxim continually impressed on medical students, for dying of such a complaint was savage. "But in Africa this terrible death is quite common," Schweitzer noted. "There are few negroes who have not, as boys, seen a man rolling in the sand of his hut and howling with agony till death comes to release him." In consequence, in the region around Andende, whenever a man felt that his rupture was a strangulated one, he begged his friends to bring him to Schweitzer's jungle hospital.

So, Schweitzer concluded, "from my own experience and from that of all colonial doctors I can say that a single doctor out here with the most modest equipment means very much for very many people. Simply with quinine and arsenic for malaria, with novarsenobenzol for the various ulcerating sores which produce diseases, with emetine to cure dysentery and with enough skill and equipment to deal with the most important operations, he can in a single year free from the tyranny of suffering and death hundreds of people who would otherwise have had to succumb to their fate in despair."

World War I added a new emotional urgency to his belief that his whole generation was living in an era of spiritual decline. "With the outbreak of war the problems of civilisation and ethics had taken on a new urgency and a cruel reality," he wrote. "The war was a sign that our civilization had failed." *We*

Epigones no longer seemed an adequate title for his projected book. "Why only a critique of culture?" he asked. "Why should I limit myself to an analysis of the *epigones*, those unsuccessful imitators of the past?" The times urgently demanded something much more constructive. The result was his magisterial *Civilisation and Ethics*.

Schweitzer wrote this book, which was not published until 1923, in French Equatorial Africa between 1914 and 1917. But he pinned down yet more precisely when its central notion of "reverence for life" first occurred to him. In 1915, after a long period of pessimistic reflection on the possibilities of some renewal of civilization, Schweitzer was obliged to make a long trip along the river Ogowe. In September he learned that a Swiss missionary had fallen ill at the mission station in N'Gômô, some two hundred kilometers upstream. To attend him, Schweitzer boarded an ancient steamboat that was towing heavily laden scows. It was the dry season, and the boat had to feel its way through huge sandbanks. Sitting in one of the scows, Schweitzer was still brooding on the problem of how a civilization might be brought into existence with a greater moral depth than the one he had lived in. Disconnected sentences filled the page of his notebook. As he remembered, "Weariness and a sense of despair paralysed my thinking."

At sunset on the third day the convoy neared the village of Igendja, sailing past an island set in the middle of the wide river. On a sandbank to the west, four hippopotami and their little ones were plodding in the same direction. Watching them, Schweitzer underwent an almost mystical experience, which came to him "as if in a dream." He realized that their lives demanded the same reverence as his. "Suddenly, in my great weariness and in my discouragement, the words 'reverence for life' came into my mind," he wrote. "I did not remember ever having read or heard them. I then realised that they contained the solution to the problem which had so much pre-occupied me."

From this notion Schweitzer eventually developed an equally mystical conception of mankind's fusion with the eternal being. As a result, he continually called upon his fellow men and women to determine rightly their proper mode of life in such a total universe, to ask themselves what were their duties not only with regard to each other, but also with regard to the natural world.

Schweitzer often repeated his belief that any religion unpurified by reason could result only in disharmony, superficiality, and, eventually, spiritual death. But, for him, reason was not "merely ordinary, superficial reflection." Nor was mysticism irrational. As he insisted to his friend Oskar Kraus (in a letter of November 18, 1925), "Mysticism is not a scientific form of knowledge in my view. But it is not in consequence for me a decadent form of philosophy. Rather it is the evidence that in its final knowable form our worldview is an 'act of thought,' not a logical operation." And as he declared in his farewell Strasbourg sermon of March 9, 1913, for him reason signified "the life of the spirit which, as it works out the path of our lives, shines from within us and attempts to illuminate the world and everything in it—the riddle of existence, the purpose and destiny of human life." Now his own reason seemed to have brought precisely such an insight into the riddle of life.

Schweitzer became obsessed with working out the implications and the meaning of reverence for life. In 1932 his friend Romain Rolland invited him to participate in a congress at Geneva. Schweitzer refused. In a letter of September 24, he told Rolland that he was haunted by the fear of dying before he had fully formulated his theory of respect for life, for he saw it as "the leaven of a new spirituality." In consequence, a volume whose title, *Civilisation and Ethics*, seems to beckon the reader into a dusty world actually opens up the soul of a man obsessed with the tragic nature of life and desperate to find some solution to it.

At the end of his autobiography, Schweitzer spoke of a curious conflict in his childhood. He had, he asserted, been a happy boy; but he continually wondered if he had the right to accept that gift of happiness. Should not he too have suffered as much as the world seemed to suffer? In *Civilisation and Ethics* the same tension returns. Sometimes one experiences moments of exaltation, he wrote, when the light of spring, the trees and flowers, the clouds, or the undulating harvest stimulate and delight. But the exaltation passes. Horrible dissonances and cacophony replace music. The beauty of nature is marred by the suffering one discerns on every side. And the moment one most respects life is the moment when this suffering becomes most strident.

Some of Schweitzer's apparently most casual writings, as when he is simply describing his life in Africa, are undergirded by these grim convictions. His book *On the Edge of the Primeval Forest* describes a visit to the home at Samkita of an Alsatian missionary couple named Morel. "Samkita," wrote Schweitzer, "is a place of leopards." One day a marauding leopard had broken into the Morels' henhouse. Killing merely to drink blood, the leopard left twenty-two hens dead, their breasts torn open. The Morels filled the body of one of them with strychnine and left it lying in front of the henhouse door. Two hours later, the leopard returned and devoured it. While the beast lay writhing in agony, Mr. Morel shot it dead.

As far as tame animals were concerned, Schweitzer's jungle hospital attempted some reconciliation amid this savage world. "We have twenty-five sheep and goats," he told one correspondent. "They are not killed, but die a natural death. In addition we have a pelican which lives on a tree in front of my room." The pelican was a friend of a nanny goat and her baby. Apart from these, "Poor dogs abandoned by the natives find their way to our hospital and stay with us." The dogs and monkeys (at the time of writing, Schweitzer said he was caring for five chimpanzees as well as eight "ordinary monkeys") readily made friends with each other. He himself became virtually a vegetarian—though not without difficulty. As he told a Viennese correspondent, Frau Evi Solny, in 1964, the great problem of whether we should kill beasts to eat them took a long time to formulate itself. It seemed not at all considered in the Bible or by philosophers. But for his part, Schweitzer had increasingly ceased to eat meat.

But Schweitzer also knew about African "leopard-men," men deluded into thinking themselves leopards and possessed with a compulsion to kill not animals, but their fellow men.

Going about on all fours, they would tie leopards' claws or iron claws to their hands and feet, and with these tear the arteries from their vicims' necks exactly as a leopard would. He knew of other men who would bite their fellows to death. As his African helper Joseph put it, "A leopard's bite is bad; worse is the bite of a poisonous snake; still worse is a monkey's bite; but the worst bite of all is that of a man."

So Schweitzer movingly wrote in 1952, "The world offers us the disconcerting spectacle of the will for life in conflict with itself. One existence maintains itself at the expense of another. The world is horror amidst magnificence, absurdity amidst the understandable, suffering amidst joy."

Schweitzer's was an ethic which, in part under the influence of Indian and Chinese as well as Christian thought, took in the whole cosmos and not simply human relations. Animals, plants, and the whole environment had, so to speak, rights which mankind needed to revere. As Schweitzer expressed one of his quasi-rational, quasi-mystical convictions in *Civilisation and Ethics*, "I am life which wishes to live, surrounded by life which wishes to live." Since every created thing desires to live, that desire must be respected. And from that it follows that every suffering being demands compassion.

The delay in publishing *Civilisation and Ethics* was due in part to the fact that Schweitzer had left the manuscript behind in Africa. For this reason, his first public utterances on reverence for life occurred in the pulpit of Saint-Nicolas, Strasbourg, on the last two Sundays of February 1919. From the same pulpit in the following month he attempted to expound the remarkable passage in the New Testament in which Saint Paul describes the whole of creation as suffering. These ideas were further developed in Schweitzer's thinking at Lambaréné and in his attempts to grapple with the philosophy of Kant, the fruits of which he next set out in a series of lectures in Sweden.

Following his by-now habitual pattern of attempting a massive research of the views of his predecessors in any intellectual field, Schweitzer here abjured his hitherto normal habit of discrediting them. On the contrary, his *Civilisation and Ethics* includes a profound admiration, for example, for the Chinese sage Meng-Tzu, whose aphorisms date back as far as the fourth and third centuries. The Confucian and Buddhist teachings on the rapport of mankind with nature also drew his praise. Schweitzer was deeply impressed by the rules of *The Book of Rewards and Punishments* (which originated at the time of the Sung dynasty of A.D. 960 to 1227). Among its maxims, one is instructed not to hurt even worms and insects, plants and trees. From among its stories Schweitzer delightedly quoted for example the tale of Taso-Pin, who lived in a ruined house. When his children beseeched him to have it mended, Taso-Pin answered with the argument that in winter the cracks between the walls, the tiles, and the stones sheltered all kinds of living creatures from the cold. Schweitzer regretted only that Chinese thinking along these lines had all too soon come to a standstill, its sages rightly clinging to the traditions of antiquity about love for living creatures but failing to develop them further.

In 1934 Schweitzer's book on the great thinkers of India pointed approvingly to their insistence on compassion for all living things and mankind's obligation to abstain from causing any arbitrary harm to them. But Schweitzer was not uncritical even of those whom he most admired. Where he disagreed with these Indian thinkers of antiquity was, first, philosophically, for he was rejecting what he saw as their absolute negation of personal life. Second, Indian ethics were, in his view, unsatisfactory for being likewise negative. Indian ethical writers commanded only a compassionate refusal to kill or harm animals without going on to commend the virtue of compassionately helping them. Tibetan Buddhists also were condemned in Schweitzer's *Indian Thought and Its Developments* for the superficial way in which they obeyed the command of not killing living creatures simply by abstaining from bloody sacrifices, whereas they would painfully suffocate to death an animal of their herds if they desired to eat its meat.

Among those he least admired were ethical philosophers who seemed to have no notion that animals had the remotest rights, treating only the relationships between human beings. In

Schweitzer's thinking, no gulf existed between human beings and the natural world. In his Strasbourg sermons, as in his *Civilisation and Ethics*, he himself repeatedly spoke of human life as a participation in the lives of others. "We live in the world, and the world lives in us," he preached. There is a "mysticism of the ethical identity fused with Being," he wrote.

Part of Schweitzer's uniqueness in this field derives from his restless quest to unify the many facets of his own thought and personality. Though he was rigorous in examining and evaluating the philosophy of ethics, at base his own ethic had a religious and specifically Christian foundation. As he wrote to his friend Dr. Hans Bauer in 1923, "It is necessary to draw attention to the profoundly religious character of my philosophical thinking. I show how thinking which seeks to be profound inevitably becomes religious and ethical." He went so far as to insist that reverence for life was the only basis of "true piety, which presents itself under that formula at its most elementary and its most profound."

Schweitzer's grand aim was to integrate his philosophy of civilization with his religious outlook and to combine his assessment of nature with his view of culture. In one sense, the amalgam at least of his mysticism and his theory of respect for life ought to have been simple. In truth, Schweitzer never satisfactorily put all these notions together, so that while he continually talked about the projected third volume of his philosophy of civilization, at his death all that he left were fragmentary pages.

In 1917, interned first at Garaison and then at Saint-Rémy-de-Provence, he devoted much of his time to this same problem—though, as he himself probably realized, what he wrote during that trying time was too much conditioned by the prevailing social and intellectual attitudes to be a definitive statement of his views. This internment might well serve as an image of the rest of Schweitzer's life. Always Schweitzer lived in constrained circumstances, into which he crammed as much as he could of music, writing, raising money, and practical medicine. A note in the margin of a manuscript of the unfinished Part Three of his *Civilisation and Ethics* reads:

In the train from Paris, 16 July 1932, looking for Uncle Charles who has just passed his holidays at Gunsbach.... At last I can again consecrate myself to working on the mysticism of respect for life. At Lambaréné in October 1931 I had to interrupt this to prepare my talk on Goethe. Then it was time for concerts: Germany—Holland—England—Scotland—Germany. Today I can thus start again concentrating on the work.

A further difficulty was the gigantic nature of the task he had set himself. Respect for life alone, he recognized, was not a totally satisfactory basis for the whole of ethics. It constituted, he averred, only the choir, so to speak, of a great cathedral that had still to be built. In addition, Schweitzer was widely bestriding disparate cultures—stepping outside the Western civilization that had bred him, and that usually decisively separated religion and philosophy into Greek, Chinese, and Indian thought, in which the distinction was by no means so secure.

So his book proceeded by fits and starts, with Schweitzer abandoning one concept, and even whole projected sections of the work, in order to redefine his objectives. Throughout these vacillations he never abandoned several convictions. Schweitzer decisively rejected the negation of the world implied in Indian philosophy. He rejected the monism of both Indian and Chinese philosophy. Dualism—as found in Christianity, Judaism, and Zarathustra—seemed far closer to the truth of the universe. Striving to complete his synthesis, he was given an opportunity to publish by the invitation to deliver the Gifford Lectures of 1936 in Great Britain. Once published, his lectures seemed to the author himself incomplete and flawed.

Schweitzer attempted to summarize his whole ethical position in a lecture given in Paris on October 22, 1952, before the *Académie des Sciences Morales et Politiques*. There he first spoke of an often-repeated experience in his jungle hospital. Schweitzer would ask a walking patient to help one confined to his bed, only to have his request refused on the grounds that the more seriously ill man was of a different tribe and therefore "not a brother to me." No amount of persuasion could get the first patient to change his mind. Schweitzer would have to give up, deciding that he was dealing with what he described as "primitive people."

As against this, Schweitzer set the notion of the solidarity of humanity. Such Chinese thinkers as Lao-tzu (born in 604 B.C.), Confucius (born some fifty years later), Meng-tzu (who lived from 371 to 289 B.C.), and the fourth-century B.C. thinker Chuang-tzu all had promulgated a much greater concept of the solidarity of mankind. So had the eighth-century B.C. Jewish prophets Amos, Hosea, and Isaiah. And through the teachings of Jesus and Saint Paul, the idea that human beings had an obligation toward all other human beings became an integral part of the Christian ethic.

In this Paris lecture, he once more insisted, as he always had done, that by no means every ethical writer of the past had reached such moral heights. Schweitzer by now had further criticisms to make of one of them. Though in their metaphysic of existence the Brahman, Buddhist, and Hindu thinkers of India embraced the brotherhood of all beings, he pointed out that many of their traditions in practice allowed some men and women to elevate themselves over their fellow human beings. In the seventh century B.C., Zarathustra similarly made a false distinction between those who (like himself) believed in Ormazd, god of light and goodness, and those unbelievers who remained dominated by demons. Plato and Aristotle, along with their fellow philosophers of the classical age of Greece, were likewise all too ready to consign all but free Greeks to a lower order of being, and only with Stoicism and Epicureanism were all men and women seen as equal. Schweitzer hailed the Stoic Panaetius, in particular, as in this respect a prophet of humanism.

Schweitzer postulated that the development of ethics proceeded best in the teachings of those who affirmed the world, rather than among world deniers such as the thinkers of India (the sacred texts of the Upanishads excepted) and of early and medieval Christianity. Denial of the world, he argued, such as is found in Samkhyan, Jainist, and Buddhist metaphysics, readily enables a believer to consider that his or her own salvation is all that matters. These religions thus develop an ethic based on metaphysics rather than compassion. Against these teachers Schweitzer aligned himself with world affirmers such as the Chinese thinkers, the Hebrew prophets, Zarathustra, and some of the European philosophers of the Renaissance and modern times.

Curiously enough, in *Indian Thought and Its Development* Schweitzer had been more appreciative of Jainism, quoting for instance the *Ayaramgasutta*, a Jain text of the third or fourth century B.C.:

> All saints and lords in the past, in the present and in the future speak, teach, announce and explain thus: one may not kill, ill-treat, insult, torment or persecute any form of life, any kind of creature, anything with a soul or any kind of being. This pure, eternal and enduring commandment of religion has been proclaimed by those wise ones who understand the world.

Schweitzer commented that "the expression of the command not to kill or harm is one of the greatest events in the spiritual history of mankind." Indian thought, he observed, had made the tremendous discovery that ethics knows no bounds. "As far as we know," he added, "this is proclaimed clearly for the first time in Jainism." The fault of Jainism, as he saw it, was to assume that the absolute command not to kill could be carried out fully. Jains thus passed by the central problem posed by an ethic of reverence for life as if it simply did not exist.

Buddha came off less lightly than the Jains. Schweitzer recounts the Buddhist view that once a man has sunk into a non-human form of existence, it was scarcely possible for him to be born again as a man, since the lower forms of being only kill each other and know nothing of good deeds. He quoted with disapproval Buddha's saying that if a yoke with a single opening is flung into the sea, and in that sea a one-eyed turtle rises to the surface only once in a hundred years, there is a far greater probability that the one-eyed turtle should in time put its neck into the yoke than that the fool who has entered into a lower form of existence should ever again achieve the existence of a human being.

In 1952 Schweitzer was content merely to summarize rather than criticize these early attempts to create a religious ethic. He then set himself to analyze the way in which early Christianity seemed able both to deny and to affirm the world. In proclaiming the imminent transformation of the world into the kingdom of God, Jesus encouraged his followers to renounce worldly matters—but not to renounce their obligations to their fellows. When the kingdom of God did not come, Christianity increasingly ceased to affirm the untransformed world. As Schweitzer put it, there was no enthusiastic affirmation of the world that could have brought in the new world.

Christians only learned to affirm the world again, Schweitzer believed, with the Renaissance. "From this marriage between Christianity and the joyful affirmation of the world at the Renaissance," he told the *Académie*, "the civilisation in which we live was born." Its most remarkable intellectual fathers were for him Erasmus and Hugo Grotius. It is, Schweitzer declared, a civilization which we now have to maintain and to perfect.

Even so, the battle for a true ethic was not entirely won at the Renaissance, said Schweitzer. Teachers of the Enlightenment such as David Hartley, Baron d'Holbach, Helvétius, and Jeremy Bentham put forward the erroneous notion that altruism was but another form of egotism, since loving others was necessary to ensure love for oneself. Only under the logic of Immanuel Kant and David Hume was it once again realized that ethics had its own absolute authority and could not be reduced to utilitarianism. The supremacy of compassion could once more be reaffirmed. And this compassion, said Schweitzer, "constantly demands the impossible of us, asking us to open our care to the point where it even endangers our own existence."

But Kant, from the point of view of Schweitzer, had a far too limited notion of the scope of ethics, confining it to the duties of human beings to each other and excluding the duties of men and women to nonhuman creatures. Against this, Schweitzer's *Civilisation and Ethics* argued, in Kantian terms, that the absolute and the universal belong together: "If there really is a fundamental principle of ethics, it must somehow refer to the relation of men and women to life in all of its manifestations." In failing to realize this, Kant, Schweitzer caustically observed, "had erected behind an imposing façade only a tenement house."

Schweitzer acknowledged that occasionally Bentham had admitted that to be merciful to animals is inherently right. But, for the most part, Bentham's principal attitude toward animals was summed up in the consideration that cruelty begets cruelty, and that unkindness to the animal kingdom could lead us to unkindness toward our fellow humans. In short, Bentham's own ethic remained anthropocentric.

In universalizing human self-devotion, such moral philosophers, asserted Schweitzer, were like a housewife who has scrubbed a room and then takes good care to keep out the dog, in case its paw prints undo her work. "So European thinkers make sure that no animals run around in their ethics." At least, he admitted, Kant had not sunk to the level of Descartes, who asserted that animals were mere machines. Schweitzer, by contrast, even discerned feelings of compassion in the animal kingdom. A crippled bird, he argued, would be left enough crumbs by its fellow sparrows. At the jungle hospital Schweitzer created at Lambaréné, whenever he adopted an orphaned monkey he found no difficulty in persuading one of the already resident monkeys to become its foster parent.

At this point, Schweitzer added his own notion that the demand for complete solidarity not just with our fellow human beings but also with the whole of nature is also a religious one. The principle of caring, he declared, "no longer permits us to be preoccupied solely with human beings but demands that we behave in the same way to all other living beings." They too, he affirmed, are like us in sharing the aspiration to happiness, the fear of suffering, and the dread of extermination. "Brooding on life," he concluded, "I find myself obliged to reverence all desire for life that surrounds me as equal to my own and equally valuable and mysterious." Thus we enter into a spiritual relationship with the whole created world. His lecture ended with, "By reverencing life we become religious in an elementary, profound and living way."

Yet, Schweitzer realized, the need simply to eat, let alone to find space to live in the world, to build towns and cities, and to develop the commerce of the modern world inflicted unavoidable damage on nature, bending it to the will of human beings, sometimes necessarily destroying it. Aware of this conflict between his absolute of "reverence for life" and the demands of daily life, Schweitzer never fully reconciled the two. The logical contradiction between his theory and his practice proved insoluble. It was not possible to behave according to Schweitzer's own maxim of respecting every desire for life as equally as one's own. The problem of eschatology, which he set out in his *Quest* and in his *Mysticism of Paul the Apostle*, had here a practical relevance too. As he put it in the latter book, having abandoned the notion of a decisive change in the conditions of earthly life, we have come to accept suffering and evil as inherent in nature.

Schweitzer was thus well aware that his ethic of reverence for life could not be applied to the whole of nature in any absolute fashion. Choices had to be made by each individual between maintaining or destroying life; but that choice must be made responsibly. Tensions and conflicts between various rights and between mankind and nature were inevitable. But Schweitzer abhorred the idea of basing such essentially moral choices simply on selfishness or worse, simply on the profit motive, and he viewed ecological irresponsibility with horror. He protested bullfights and cockfighting openly, along with falconing and the hunting of animals for mere pleasure. He attacked the brutality of many slaughterhouses. He was appalled by the cries of thirsty beasts in railway trucks. He deplored the way many animals went to a painful death through unskillful hands in kitchens. He raged against the sufferings of animals subjected to the cruel play of children.

As early as the 1920s, Schweitzer was also expressing his concern about experiments on animals by surgery, by drugs, or by inoculating them with diseases. No one should have a quiet conscience merely because such experiments might in general have worthy results. "Every single experiment needs to be examined, to ask whether one should demand of this animal its sacrifice for humans," he insisted. If an experiment went for-ward, every care should be taken to mitigate pain. How often had outrages taken place when scientists failed to administer an anestheic to an animal, simply in order to save time and trouble? How often did other scientists subject animals to torture merely to demonstrate what was already general knowledge? Since every human being stood to benefit from such experiments, every single one of us was implicated in them. "Not a single one of us," said Schweitzer, "should allow any preventable pain to be inflicted, even though the responsibility for inflicting that pain is not ours."

Schweitzer made now the radical suggestion that because through such often-painful experiments animals had contribut-ed so much to mankind, a new bond of solidarity had been established between them and human beings. In consequence, men and women were obliged to do every possible good to all animals. "Whenever I help a needy insect, I am merely attempt-ing to discharge a little of the continually growing debt of mankind to the animal kingdom," he averred.

Yet in the end Schweitzer himself was obliged to fall back on the concept of different stages of values—between plants, ani-mals, and humankind—a resort which contradicted his insis-tence in *My Life and Thought* that reverence for life allowed "no differentation between evolved lives and inferior lives." Empiri-cally we are often obliged to destroy life. Mankind was thus, Schweitzer believed, continually guilty. In his address of 1952 to the Paris *Académie*, he asserted that "it behooves each of us to judge whether we find ourselves in the ineluctable necessity of causing suffering and killing, and to resign ourselves to becom-ing of necessity guilty. We must seek pardon by not passing by any possible occasion to succor living beings."

Schweitzer's philosophy of ethics was thus inseparable from his practical and personal life. In his African jungle hospital he was surrounded by animals whose wounds he had tended, yet he fed them on other animals and fish. He perceived in verte-brates and invertebrates alike moments of joy and fear, decisive-ly rejecting the writings of those who saw these creatures as mere machines. His autobiography courted ridicule by confessing that when he constructed a new building for his hospital, before putting beams into the ground he would carefully pick out of the holes any insects or frogs. He even replanted the young palm trees that had to be removed to make way for his own house.

This was part of his definition of a true human being. Schweitzer clearly believed that only by attempting to live according to the theory of reverence for life was one completely human. His *Civilisation and Ethics* described such a human being: "He breaks no leaf from a tree, plucks no flower and is careful to crush no insect under his feet. Working by the lamp of a summer evening, he prefers to keep his window closed, breathing stifling air before seeing insect after insect fall on his table with singed wings. After rain he will walk along a road, see an earthworm that has gone astray and help it from the stones onto the grass, so that the rising sun will not dry it up. Coming upon an insect that has fallen into a puddle, he will pause to save it by extending to it a stalk or leaf."

Schweitzer remained insistent that every single time a person inflicted damage on another life, he or she should ponder precisely why the deed was unavoidable and how little harm was necessary. A peasant might need to chop down millions of flowers to feed his beasts. If on his way home he switched the head off one more flower merely for pleasure, he had committed a crime against life that was indefensible.

In acknowledging the contradictions at the heart of the universe as he understood it, Schweitzer also was generous in his praise of a distinguished contemporary from the Indian traditions. The English version of his *Indian Thought and Its Development* quoted Mahatma Gandhi as observing that the fate of animals was probably sadder in his own country than anywhere else in the world. Gandhi's own principles demanded complete compassion for animals rather than merely the common Hindu commandment against killing or hurting them. He offended many of his Hindu adherents when he ended the sufferings of a calf in prolonged agony by giving it poison.

By such actions, said Schweitzer, Gandhi was compelling Indian ethics to come to grips with reality. With a similarly heavy heart, Schweitzer equally refused to exclude reality from his own ethic of reverence for life. Ethics, he had reluctantly come to believe, involves conflicts that require us to make what can only be subjective decisions. "We are living truthfully when we experience these conflicts in all their profundity," he declared. "The good conscience," he added, "is the invention of the devil."

CHAPTER 8

◆

Internment, Despair, and Resurrection

In the late summer of 1914 World War I broke out and immediately created an absurdly difficult situation for the Schweitzers in French Equatorial Africa. "As Alsatians my wife and I were German nationals," Schweitzer explained. "This fact had not barred us from the French colony of Gabon, nor had it kept me from establishing a hospital there. But now, since we were at war, my wife and I were regarded as enemy aliens—and treated as such." So were their fellow Alsatians Monsieur and Madame Morel, who had gone to Gabon to work in 1908 and were to remain as missionaries until 1935.

Initially these foreigners were allowed to remain in their own homes but were denied all contact with either other Europeans or Africans. Four African soldiers and an African superior officer kept guard at the door. Schweitzer kept his spirits high by devoting his energies to working on his book about the spiritual decline of Western civilization. But he and Hélène were not without friends. Their Parisian allies, particularly an incensed Charles-Marie Widor, entreated the French government not to treat them in this fashion; more, both the Europeans and the

Africans in and around Andende vigorously complained that interning Schweitzer robbed them of their sole doctor. In November the internment was lifted.

A further and increasingly worsening problem was how to ensure the supply of sufficient medical supplies. Strasbourg now lay in enemy territory, and the parishioners, pastors, and friends who had kept Schweitzer's coffers and medicine chests adequately filled could no longer be reached. The professor of medicine who had initially stocked Schweitzer with most of his medicines was equally out of touch. Albert took the risk of running into debt to buy further supplies. He and Hélène took to eating monkey flesh. They reduced costs by paying Joseph Azowani less, at which Joseph resigned, thus adding to the work of the already overburdened and increasingly exhausted Schweitzers.

The two struggled on until September 1917. Albert Schweitzer took comfort from the fact that at least he could pursue his intellectual work as a source of what he called "moral health" and as a respite from fighting all day against the unreliability of his African helpers and the attacks of insects. "Once again one becomes a human being," he wrote. He also set himself the impossible task of explaining to his black congregations why the white followers of the Prince of Peace could have turned on each other savagely.

Life back home in Alsace was becoming increasingly dangerous. Harry Bresslau and his family were obliged to escape to comparative safety farther inside Germany. Then, on July 3, 1916, Schweitzer's parents walked to the home of a friend in Walbach. It was raining, and on their way home, as they rounded a bend under their umbrellas, two German cavalrymen galloped past them. A moment later, a third cavalryman, his horse out of control, crashed into Schweitzer's mother and flung her to the ground. She was carried home on a hay cart, foaming at the mouth and with her skull fractured. The combined skills of two doctors, one from Strasbourg, the other from Sulzbach, failed to save her, and she died at two o'clock the following morning.

Communications were so slow that only on August 15 did

Albert Schweitzer write to his father about this, a letter which he partially reprinted in his *Out of My Life and Thought:* "I am writing to say that I know that mother lies in the graveyard." Clearly, in his own distressed state of mind he had long feared some such calamity, for he added that as he heard the siren of the ship in the distance, he knew it brought bad news. His mother's portrait was on the wall of his room, and he and Hélène decorated it with palm fronds and olive blossoms. "I am still too shattered to make sense of it all, and in my mind's eye I can see the corner of the graveyard in all its summer beauty," he told Louis Schweitzer. "I think of what it will be like when Hélène and I greet her on our return home."

In October, the two of them joined the Morels for a stay by the sea at Cap Lopez, helped by a timber merchant who lent them one of his houses. Swimming, catching fish, caring for the collection of pet animals they had brought along from Andende, studying, and writing, the Schweitzers gradually began to recover their former strengths. They stayed until the following fateful summer, Albert managing to rent the house with the approval and some of the money of the Paris Evangelical Missionary Society on condition that any passing missionaries could stay there.

They had scarcely returned to Andende when the newly formed French government of Georges Clemenceau turned on aliens living in the French colonies on the grounds that security there was far too lax. Once again they were to be interned, and all prisoners from the west coast of French Equatorial Africa were ordered to be transferred to Bordeaux. The Schweitzers were allowed to take only 110 pounds of luggage and were told to pack immediately. "Fortunately our boat for Europe was late," recalled Schweitzer, "giving us time to pack and store most of our belongings at the mission stations." He judged that the philosophical sketches he had written in German almost certainly would be confiscated, so he summarized the contents in French and begged an American missionary at Lambaréné to care for the original. The American frankly confessed to Schweitzer that he would gladly have thrown the parcel of manuscripts into the river Ogowe, since he considered philosophy not simply unnecessary, but positively harmful. "But out of Christian love he agreed to look after them for me till the end of the war," noted a thankful Schweitzer. "I was thus able to begin my enforced trip to Bordeaux with some peace of mind."

There is a certain historical irony about the way Schweitzer was treated by the French at this time, for his family had been unanimously opposed to the German annexation of Alsace in 1871. Two brothers of Schweitzer's father had without hesitation opted to live in France and moved to Paris. Even Schweitzer's father, working as a pastor in Gunsbach, showed a slightly uncharitable coolness to German immigrants, and indeed throughout his life he warmed only to a few of their families.

A timber merchant exchanged French bank notes for Schweitzer's supply of gold, and Albert and Hélène sewed them into their clothing. Even now, with time running out, Albert found time to operate on the strangulated hernia of an African. Then they boarded the *Afrique* for Europe. The last man to say good-bye to them was the superior of the local Roman Catholic mission. The Schweitzers and he promised to meet again but never did, for the father superior was lost at sea later, sailing himself on the *Afrique* when it was sunk in the Bay of Biscay.

Reaching Bordeaux in November, Albert and Hélène Schweitzer were interned alongside some refugees in a former army transit camp and barracks at 136, rue de Belleville. Although they managed to obtain some warmer clothing, both Hélène and Albert suffered miserably from the cold weather, and before the year was out both of them had fallen ill with dysentery. Worse, Hélène also contracted tuberculosis—an illness which, along with the disability that had resulted from her skiing accident, was to prevent her ever again being able to work permanently with Albert in his missionary hospitals.

Their next prison was a large internment camp at Garaison, sixteen kilometers north of Lannemezan in the Hautes-Pyrénées. The prefect of the *département* of the Gironde telegraphed the prefect of the *département* of Hautes-Pyrénées, declaring that the pair were German suspects who should be transferred to the new camp. When they arrived, Albert ironically was amused that the name of the camp derived from the local patois word for *healing*, since Garaison in the Middle Ages had been a pilgrimage center whose miraculous cures led to the establishment of a health resort.

A fine sixteenth-century chapel remained from the previous usage of the camp. Now its numerous buildings housed seventeen hundred Austro-German civilians, prisoners of war from France and its colonies. Schweitzer was the only doctor of medicine among the men, women, and children he discovered interned there; yet initially the camp director, a retired colonial official and theosophist named Vecchi, refused him permission to tend the sick. According to Schweitzer himself, this was not mere insensitivity. Vecchi, he avowed, "fulfilled his job with justice and kindliness." But the medical supervision of the camp was the duty of an elderly country doctor of the region, and Vecchi liked to play things by the book. He soon relented. "After a few weeks the director decided that it would be only fair to give the camp the benefit of my profession as a doctor," recalled Schweitzer. "He put an office at my disposal and allotted living quarters to my wife and me."

So Schweitzer became a doctor again—and also a philosopher, for in case he never got back his philosophical sketches from his American friend in Lambaréné, he began to draft his book anew. After a fashion he also once more began to practice as an organist, by a remarkable coincidence. Before being transported from Andende Schweitzer had given some drugs to a fellow deportee named Dahomey, who in turn had handed them over to the sick wife of a French engineer. Now that same engineer learned that Schweitzer was interned in Garaison and made him a table on which, using the floor as an imaginary pedal board, Schweitzer practiced Bach fugues and Widor's Sixth Symphony for the organ.

A fellow internee sketched a silhouette of the doctor practicing on his imaginary organ. Schweitzer himself wrote to his sister Adèle Woytt in 1918, "Tell old Münch that never a day goes by without my thinking of him, that I would profoundly rejoice to see him again and that I am exercising my fingers admirably by practising the organ on a table." He added that occasionally he was also able to play on an old harmonium.

Life moderately improved. The Bresslau family managed to send the Schweitzers money. When their Parisian allies persuaded the authorities to give the Schweitzers the right to chose which camp they should be confined in, the two of them decided to stay at Garaison. At Schweitzer's request, Director Vecchi had used his influence to prevent a transfer, for Schweitzer had told him that the climate at Garaison, situated halfway up the mountain, was vital if the doctor and his wife were to recover from the anemia they had contracted in Gabon. In another letter, written on Christmas Eve of 1917, Schweitzer added that he also would like to stay there "out of duty," rejecting the offer of living in a locality somewhere in the Midi between Bordeaux and Toulouse, since he had been authorized to offer his medical services to the other internees.

But the Schweitzers' situation remained a delicate one. Vecchi's attempts to keep them at Garaison seemed increasingly doomed to failure. Now that Albert and Hélène had been so decisively identified as French Alsatians, the prefect was adamant that they could no longer stay in a camp designed for Austro-Germans. They were offered the choice of two camps reserved exclusively for prisoners from Alsace-Lorraine, one at Luçon in the Vendée, the other at Saint-Rémy-de-Provence. Both camps offered a remarkable degree of freedom.

Internment in the Vendée seemed insufferable to Albert Schweitzer, for he was even more anxious about his wife's failing strength than he was about his own. "Madame Schweitzer and I have used up our health in looking after the sick of French Equatorial lands," he told the director, who alone could appeal to the authorities on their behalf. "Her physical state will not permit her to accompany me to Luçon in the Vendée. I therefore beg them to authorize me to stay beside her at Garaison until the day she is allowed to go home, for she needs the care which a colonial doctor can give her." In uttering such a prayer, he insisted, he could not be asking too much of France. "It would be tragic if my wife, who for years has devoted herself to sick French people in Gabon and who has sacrificed her health for them must be deprived of the care she needs because of this activity."

Two days later, on January 26, 1918, Vecchi wrote again to the prefect of the Hautes-Pyrénées arguing against this second offer allowing the Schweitzers the possibility of living in France in comparative freedom. Apart from the importance of the beneficial air of Garaison for the health of both internees, the director wrote that if the German government learned that the two had been set virtually at liberty, they would inevitably take reprisals against Schweitzer's family in Alsace. The Germans suspected Albert Schweitzer precisely because of all that he had achieved for French art and literature, and above all because he had established his humanitarian work in a French colony. Finally, wrote Vecchi, the doctor's services were particularly appreciated at Garaison by those internees suffering from paludism (malaria) and dysentery contracted in the colonies. Again Vecchi wrote in vain.

Albert now anxiously begged Vecchi to enquire about Saint-Rémy-de-Provence. On February 15 the director of this camp sent back a description of the establishment. It was installed, he said, some 200 meters above the town in the former convent of Saint-Paul-de-Mausole, which had once cared for the mentally ill and those suffering from nervous disorders. He praised the pure air, the clean water, and the excellent climate of the region, a climate, he wrote, "virtually that of Nice." The camp, he said, had space for 150 internees, though at that moment it housed only 105, all from Alsace-Lorraine. Nearly every one was a member of the liberal professions—priests, medical men, and so on. Each household or individual was housed separately. Twice a week supervised excursions into the surrounding countryside took place, and the internees could daily walk in a pretty park shaded by huge pines and other trees.

The post was collected four times a month, said the director. As for food, it consisted of a daily ration per person of 300 grams of bread, supplemented with 200 grams of meat on Sundays, Tuesdays, and Thursdays. The prisoners also were given a kilo of potatoes, dried vegetables, as well as 200 grams of fresh ones, along with pâté or rice. Other foodstuffs, as well as wine and beer, were available in a canteen for those who wanted to supplement these rations. What is more, everything was supplied free of charge. Whatever money the internees brought was carefully locked away; they were given tokens to pay for their daily needs; and their own cash would be returned in full once they were released.

The director's letter ended, "If M. Schweitzer comes to Saint-Rémy I shall remember that you told me that he has rendered service in the French Congo and I shall do everything in my power for him." So on March 26, Albert and Hélène said good-bye to the director of the internment camp at Garaison and the following day arrived at Saint-Rémy-de-Provence.

The moment the Schweitzers moved into the day room of their new internment camp, the room struck him, "in its unadorned and bare ugliness," as strangely familiar. Where, he asked, had he seen that iron stove and the flue pipe that crossed from end to end of the room? The answer suddenly dawned on him. "I knew them from a drawing of Van Gogh's, who had immortalised with his pen the desolate room in which we in our turn were today sitting. Like us he had suffered from the cold stone floor when the mistral blew! Like us he had walked round and round between the high walls of the garden."

Like the other prisoners, the Schweitzers were given their own room. Over the doorway was a wooden placard, inscribed, ROOM 49. DR. SCHWEITZER ALBERT 42 YEARS. MAD. SCHWEITZER HÉLÈNE 38 YEARS. CHEF DE CHAMBRE: MAD. SCHWEITZER HÉLÈNE. And in these more auspicious surroundings Hélène conceived the Schweitzers' only child.

At Saint-Rémy-de-Provence the camp already had a doctor as an inmate, so once again the director temporarily forbade Schweitzer to practice medicine. Eventually, this disappointment was relieved when the camp doctor was transferred home through an exchange of prisoners, and Albert once more was allowed to practice medicine. Soon Schweitzer was working as a doctor not only in the camp but in the surrounding villages, whose inhabitants also were suffering grievously from the privations of the long, drawn-out war. One night he was called out to visit the apparently dying grandmother of a family named Mauron. Schweitzer managed to save her life, and continued to look after her so assiduously that her husband prevailed upon the director of the internment camp to let him spend evenings dining with them. Monsieur Mauron's granddaughter Marie recalled the aura of the doctor: "Big, powerful, even massive, his wild hair irregularly brushed, calm, his whole face smiling, his regard direct, he was tall enough to dominate everyone else." She remembered that Schweitzer was deaf to insults, unostentatiously saluting anyone he passed, whether they returned his greeting or not, and eventually winning over even the most hostile of the locals. When Schweitzer once more set up a jungle hospital, the citizens of Saint-Rémy-de-Provence were generous in their financial support.

Nonetheless, the Schweitzers were unhappy. Albert was concealing his own illness from his patients. A contemporary photograph shows him sitting glumly in the high-walled garden, wearing Provençal clogs, his blouse buttoned up against the wind, his eyes peering sadly out from under a cap. As for Hélène, the savage mistral wracked her body, and she could scarcely bear the cold flagstones of the camp. Both she and her husband were physically too weak, and probably also too dispirited, to join in the recreational walks the kindly camp governor (who refused to dub his unwilling guests "prisoners" and always addressed them as "boarders") allowed his inmates.

Increasingly frequent exchanges of prisoners gave the Schweitzers some hope, and their influential French friends were assiduous in trying to persuade the authorities to add them to the lists of those to be sent home. In July they were successful. Schweitzer had taken the precaution of showing his sketches on the philosophy of civilization to the camp censor, who stamped several pages to prevent any hostile official from confiscating them on the way back to Alsace.

The returning prisoners traveled by rail from Tarascon to Zurich in Switzerland. A sign of the toll their sufferings had wreaked on the Schweitzers was that neither of them was fit enough to carry their own luggage through the scorching sun to the train. Schweitzer was deeply moved that his was carried by a crippled fellow internee. From Zurich the couple traveled on to Constance. Hélène now left her husband, allowed to take the first possible train to join the Bresslaus in Strasbourg if Albert would stay behind to complete the necessary papers. Emaciated though he was, Schweitzer spent a further day in Constance, helping the less able to complete their own papers, before reaching Strasbourg late on July 17.

Suzanne was waiting for him, along with his sister Louise, and he was installed in the rue Saint-Thomas. The following morning his father arrived. But the military passes to allow the Schweitzers back to Gunsbach proved difficult to procure. Pastor Louis returned alone, while his son and Suzi stayed in Strasbourg. The exiles joined Hélène at Louise's home in Colmar, and only at the beginning of August was the pastor able to return from Gunsbach, pick them up, and take them home.

Back in his native Alsace, Schweitzer attempted to fight off the illness and anxiety that had plagued him for so long. "Among my native hills I kept hoping, in vain, to cast off my langour, but I grew increasingly worse," he wrote. He played the organ at the forty-fourth anniversary celebration of his father's induction at Gunsbach. Since his bout of dysentery at Bordeaux, he had suffered a painful abscess in his rectum. The pain grew worse, as did an accompanying fever, and, finally, in August 1918 Albert underwent a short operation and the abscess was gone.

Coping with his internal malaise proved less easy. The mayor of Strasbourg helped by offering Schweitzer his old post at the hospital in Strasbourg, and he was also invited to take up once again his former position at the Church of Saint-Nicolas. Both offers were accepted with alacrity, for Schweitzer had no other way of supporting himself and his pregnant wife.

On October 13, 1918, Schweitzer preached his first sermon at Saint-Nicolas, Strasbourg, since his departure for Africa five and a half years earlier. It reveals, not surprisingly, the spiritual and emotional upheaval that had taken place in many during the vicious conflict that had ended with the armistice signed but two days earlier. "How homesick I have felt for this place," Schweitzer exclaimed. Then he immediately spoke of the dead choirboys of Saint-Nicolas, killed in far-off fields, who had sung the chorale from the organ loft when he said good-bye.

That same year he preached four more times in remembrance of the dead, culminating in a sermon on December 1, in which he brutally asked his congregation to remember how they had died. "They bled to death when the bullet tore into their bodies. Trapped on barbed wire they hung there for days, starving and crying for help, with no-one able to come to help them. At night they froze to death on the cold earth. Swirling currents destroyed the ships in which they sailed, so that either they had to fight against the waves until exhaustion set in or else they helplessly braced themselves against the bulwarks of the ship's hold in panic." Others, he added, survived the battlefield or the sea, only to die in agony weeks or months later in field hospitals.

All Schweitzer could offer in comfort was the vow that these dead should not be forgotten and that determination that they had not died in vain. Henceforth every barrier of nationality must be set aside. The heartless spirit in which these young lives were lost must itself be destroyed. "The inviolable law of the world from now on must be reverence for human suffering and for human life, however small and insignificant." He added that the dead had been sacrificed because of an attitude of mind that had not yet come to understand the meaning of the commandment, "Thou shalt not kill."

"Often, meeting friends returning from the front, I have observed a different expression on their faces," Schweitzer told his Strasbourg congregation on the afternoon of Sunday, December 1. "It is as if the atrocities they have seen have indelibly marked their features." Schweitzer's own features had been indelibly marked by his own experiences. So had Hélène's. She would spend hours perspiring in apparent apprehension. She was seriously underweight and as depressed as Albert was. Her depression was scarcely relieved by the birth of their daughter, Rhena, on Schweitzer's forty-fourth birthday, January 14, 1919.

Amid the rejoicing, and as he attempted to pick up the pieces of his past life, Albert felt, he said, "like a coin that had rolled away under a wardrobe and been forgotten."

Salvation came from an unexpected quarter. Nathan Söderblom was archbishop of Uppsala in Sweden. A formidable Lutheran scholar, he had for a time been pastor of the Swedish Lutheran church in Paris before taking up the post of professor of theology at Uppsala University in 1901. Between then and his consecration as archbishop in 1914, Söderblom frequently returned to Paris. Like Schweitzer, he believed in applying every possible critical faculty to the study of holy scripture, and said so in print in 1903. Like Schweitzer, he believed that there was more than one approach to religious truth, and for his own part was fascinated by Zoroastrianism among the non-Christian religions. His stature in Germany was high enough for him to be offered, in 1912, a professorship of theology at Leipzig, which he held concurrently with his professorship at Uppsala.

Schweitzer scarcely knew of Söderblom, but Söderblom had read and admired the works of Schweitzer. In 1919, he also believed that Schweitzer was still interned. At that moment Söderblom was drawing up a list of lecturers for a series at Uppsala University sponsored by the Olaus-Petri foundation. To spring Schweitzer from his supposed internment, he turned to the venerable Archbishop Randall Davidson of Canterbury, whom he supposed would have some influence over the victorious powers. In consequence, just as the Schweitzers were looking forward gloomily to a Christmas that Albert himself expected to be quite as bad as any they had experienced since the outbreak of World War I, Schweitzer received an invitation to lecture in Uppsala. His spirits were so low that he almost refused. Söderblom persuaded him to change his mind.

In his own words, Schweitzer went to Uppsala "tired, depressed and still a sick man." There he partially recovered his health and once more began to find enjoyment in work. Schweitzer offered to lecture on the philosophy of civilization, and Söderblom was so impressed with the lecture that the two men became firm friends. The day before Schweitzer was due to return to Strasbourg he and the archbishop shared an umbrella as they walked through the rainy streets of Uppsala. Schweitzer confided in Söderblom his deep financial anxieties. The astute archbishop replied that there was plenty of money to be made out of lecturing and performing organ recitals in Sweden, which after all had remained neutral and had thus not only remained comparatively prosperous during the war, but also was enjoying a postwar boom. What is more, Söderblom set about arranging the whole tour.

For six weeks from the middle of May, armed with letters of introduction from the archbishop and with his accommodations already secured, Schweitzer played and lectured throughout Sweden. "In the course of several weeks," he gratefully recalled, "I was able to collect enough money not only to repay my debts but also to save enough to continue my work at Lambaréné." Söderblom even found a publisher to put out the first edition of Schweitzer's account of his life on the edge of the primeval forest. Its translator had been one of his hostesses on the triumphant Swedish tour, Baroness Greta Lagerfeld. Schweitzer, it seemed, had recovered his ability to charm intelligent women.

Thus almost by accident and through the insight of Söderblom, not only was Schweitzer's life transformed; in addition, he had discovered a new thread in the pattern he was to weave for almost all the rest of his life. In between spells of working in the new missionary hospital he planned to set up, Schweitzer would raise money for his work by lecturing and playing the organ throughout Europe—and later in the United States.

On the Edge of the Primeval Forest captured the public's attention as none of his books had since *The Quest of the Historical Jesus*. This time too the public was truly a general one and not simply those who were committed to Christianity or studied it academically. It is easy to see why. Perhaps because Schweitzer's Swedish publisher, Lindblad, insisted on a short book that could have a general appeal, Schweitzer undammed the geniality that had been blocked up during his years of suffering.

His book recreated for Europe an exotic world. "Whoever

has seen a shark never forgets it and never mistakes it for anything else," he told his readers. "Yet the Negroes in all the ports dive for coins in spite of the sharks. The noise they make in doing so gets on the nerves even of these hyenas of the deep, so that accidents seldom happen." Schweitzer told of one diver who nonetheless remained completely silent. "Later I spotted that he was the most skilful of them all, remaining silent because his mouth was a purse which he could hardly close because of the many coins crammed into it."

He could once again make fun of himself. "The blacks are displeased with me," he wrote, "because I won't use my rifle enough. On one journey we passed an alligator sleeping in the stump of a tree which rose from the water. Instead of shooting it I simply watched it. That was more than enough for them." Schweitzer turned their complaint to his own advantage, writing passionately out of long-pondered convictions. He would not even shoot a monkey, he insisted. Those who do try to kill them usually manage only to wound three or four of them, so that they never manage to eat monkey's meat. If one does find a hunted monkey, he added, "one often discovers a poor, tiny baby monkey, clinging with pitiful cries to the body of its dead mother, who is already growing cold."

Of course, he had become accustomed to monkey's meat during privations of war, he confessed. But Darwinism took its toll here. Were men and women really descended from monkeys? If so, to eat the sweet flesh of these animals was somehow repugnant. Schweitzer quoted a white man who had told him that "eating monkeys is the first step towards cannibalism."

In later editions, the photographs of potbellied Pahouin children were touching; that of a black child sick with malaria, his stomach grotesquely swollen, infinitely moving. Here too was a photograph of the doctor's assistant, Joseph Azowani, in solar topee and white medical robe, examining the leg of a young black boy with the thatched roof of the jungle hospital in the background. Schweitzer did not pull punches in his book. He spoke of the social problems of the primeval forest—of polygamy and the sale of women—as well as those brought by the liquor of the white man. He also touched the heartstrings with his description of a wartime Christmas in the jungle in 1914. As Albert extinguished the candle on the little palm that served them as a Christmas tree, his wife asked what he thought he was doing. "It's our only one," he replied, "and we must save it for next year." She shook her head. "For next year?" There was another Christmas celebration for the Schweitzers in the primeval forest in 1915, and Albert described that too, this time the candle entirely burning itself out on the Christmas palm tree, just as the lights of civilization already had been extinguished in Europe.

Schweitzer had returned from Sweden to Strasbourg to write the book for Lindblad. It was published in Sweden under the title *Between the Water and the Jungle* and in Switzerland the following year by Paul Haupt of Bern. Beck Verlag of Munich published the German edition in 1925, and then editions appeared in New York and Britain under the inspired title *On the Edge of the Primeval Forest*.

It ended with an implicit appeal. Friends at home, said Schweitzer, attempting to dissuade him from leaving for Africa, used to affirm for him that "the natives who live in the bosom of nature are not so ill as we are and do not feel pain the way we do." Schweitzer declared that he had come to see that such statements were totally untrue. "Out there prevail most of the illnesses which we know in Europe, and many of them, the most hateful, the ones which we have taken there, bring if possible more misery than they do to us."

The native of Africa may well be regarded as a child of nature, thought Schweitzer, but to be human means to be subject to the power of that fearful lord whose name is pain. "Out there physical misery is great," he witnessed. "Have we the right to close our eyes before it, to ignore it, because the European newspapers do not speak of it?" He asked his readers to imagine what life would have been like for them over the last ten years without the slightest medical or surgical help. "We must awake out of sleep and face up to our responsibilities," he proclaimed.

Schweitzer confessed here his belief that his life's work was "to fight under far-away stars on behalf of the sick." He appealed "to the sympathy called for by Jesus and religion." He also appealed to the fundamental reasoning and elemental ideas of mankind: "We should perceive the task that needs to be done for the coloured people not as 'good works' but as a duty that cannot be shirked." In a return to the inspiration of Bartholdi's statue, he described this duty "not as benevolence but as atonement."

A sign of his return to the world of his peers was an honorary doctorate in divinity, awarded him by the faculty of theology at Zurich University in the year *On the Edge of the Primeval Forest* was published in Sweden. The following spring he was playing the organ in Barcelona at the request of his old friend Lluis Millet, accompanying the first-ever Spanish performance of Bach's *Saint Matthew Passion*. By April, he felt strong enough to resign his two posts in Strasbourg, ceasing to work in the hospital and to occupy the pulpit at Saint-Nicolas. Although he retained a room in the city in the rue de l'Ail, he now became his father's curate, living at Gunsbach, where he could work on his philosophy of civilization.

One more step on the road to recovery was needed, namely his analysis by Oscar Pfister. In the meantime, Schweitzer seemed to be appearing everywhere in those parts of the intellectual and musical world that had not been interrupted by World War I, performing and lecturing to raise enough money to rebuild his jungle hospital. And with his travels, his prestige grew. *On the Edge of the Primeval Forest* was published in Britain to coincide with lectures (delivered in French, for the most part, with the help of a carefully rehearsed interpreter) at Selly Oak College, Birmingham, on Christianity and the world religions. At Mansfield College, Oxford, he lectured on a more abstrusely titled subject, "the struggle for the ethical conception of the world in European philosophy." In Cambridge he spoke on the meaning of eschatology, and at the society for the science of religion in London his subject was the Pauline problem. During the same tour he played a series of organ recitals, billed as his "Hour of Religious Music," at Carr's Lane Chapel in Birmingham and at Christ Church, Oxford.

On these tours, Albert was determined that nothing should go wrong. The distinguished and witty biblical scholar Nathaniel Micklem was then a professor at Selly Oak College and remembered how Schweitzer sat at the organ for many hours before he was due to play, going through every bar of his music, making copious notes in the margin about the stops, and refusing every entreaty to come and eat. "I cannot imagine more meticulous preparation," wrote Micklem. Micklem also was obliged to stand in when an interpreter apparently failed to turn up. According to Micklem, Schweitzer's lecture had not been written (which is inconceivable), but it is fair comment to say, as he did, that "I got through my duty somehow, but it gave me perhaps the most exhausting hour I have ever known!"

Early in March 1922, *The Times* carried the report that "The 'hour of religious music' which is given every Tuesday in Lent in Westminster Abbey was filled this week by Dr. Albert Schweitzer, the chief living authority on the works of Bach," adding that he shortly would be performing in Sweden before returning to play on the organ he had built in Alsace. The Schweitzer legend was growing. The column reminded its readers that in French Equatorial Africa Schweitzer had practiced "on a small-pedal organ,' so that no one would expect him instantly to master the stops of the five-manual instrument in Westminster Abbey. Assisted by his wife, Schweitzer had studied them devotedly.

Lyrical is the only word to describe this supposedly factual report in *The Times*. It continued: "There is something in his quiet voice and kindly demeanour, and in the large hand in which one's own is swallowed up, that seems to come out of his playing. It is in no sense for effect. Everything is quietly in its place, with beautiful phrasing, particularly on the pedals. 'Ja, das muss so genau gespielt gewesen,' he said."

In the middle of these recitals was a hymn, during which a collection was taken up for what *The Times* called "his hospital for leprosy and sleeping sickness." Schweitzer also welcomed the fees from these lectures as a further contribution to his ambition of returning to Africa. The next two years thus saw Schweitzer energetically pursuing in Sweden, Switzerland, Prague, and Copenhagen this career as public performer in words and music. A flurry of publications in 1923 rewarded the enormous amount of intellectual work he had managed to intersperse among his other activities. And in February 1924, spurred on by Pfister's analysis, he wrote and saw published his *Memoirs of Childhood and Youth*. In the same month, he left Strasbourg for Africa, leaving Hélène behind. Permanently crippled, caring for a young daughter, she had no choice, whereas, as Albert told his niece Suzi, he felt like a fir tree, bent under the winter's snow, which had shaken it off as spring came and straightened up again.

Before he went out again to French Equatorial Africa, some provision had to be made for the well-being of Hélène and Rhena. The Schweitzers built a house at Königsfeld in the Black Forest between Villingen and Peterzell. The spot was well chosen. Not only was it surrounded by pine woods; it also was noted center of the Moravian Brethren, a pietistic group of Protestant Christians whom both Albert and Hélène admired; and it had been given over since the late nineteenth century to the followers of the Reverend Sebastian Kneipp, who had developed various forms of hydrotherapy for consumptives and sufferers from tuberculosis and related illnesses. To Hélène, it must have seemed as if she and Rhena were being committed to a temporary limbo.

There, between his tours, Albert was able to work on his books, all the while planning to leave the family for Africa. Samples of new drugs against sleeping sickness arrived from America. A young Englishman named Noel Gillespie, an Oxford student of chemistry and medicine whom he had met in Colmar two years previously, was pressing Schweitzer to take him on as an assistant. Schweitzer continually was packing crates for the journey. On February 14, 1924, Schweitzer bade good-bye to the Gunsbach parsonage and to his wife and daughter. He was met at Bordeaux by Noel Gillespie.

The *Orestes*, the Dutch cargo ship on which they sailed,

berthed unexpectedly in the Cameroons. Schweitzer transferred to the mail boat *Europa* and then reached Cap Lopez (by now know as Port-Gentil) on the African coast. The party took three days, journeying up the Ogowe on Schweitzer's old and by now battered friend, the *Alémbé*, to reach Lambaréné. Although the hospital had almost completely collapsed, the tom-toms were singing out that the doctor had returned, and soon the sick once more were swarming around the compound.

Albert Schweitzer was obliged to double up once more as builder and doctor. But his fame and the newly won renown of his task now brought further hands. The following July a young nurse from Strasbourg named Mathilde Kottmann joined Schweitzer and Noel Gillespie. Three months later, the team was reinforced by an Alsatian doctor named Victor Nessmann, who had been one of Albert's fellow students. In 1925, a Swiss doctor named Mark Lauterbourg arrived from Bern to add his resources to the missionary hospital, and the team rejoiced in autumn at the arrival of another Strasbourg nurse, a former teacher named Emma Hausknecht, who was to remain one of Schweitzer's most faithful assistants until her death in 1956.

As Schweitzer and his friends toiled to rebuild the hospital, it became increasingly clear that the site itself was inadequate for the new needs of the Africans. For one thing, several tribes had recently been transferred to the area from other parts of Gabon to work in the timber industry. Second, an epidemic of amebic dysentery struck the region, enormously increasing the medical work load. Third, leprosy and sleeping sickness had both tightened their malicious grip on the inhabitants of French Equatorial Africa since Schweitzer's last sojourn there.

Schweitzer decided to build on a more spacious site. A hillock named Adoninalongo (which means "it overlooks the tribes") was cleared at Lambaréné, and the work of creating a hospital capable of dealing with 250 patients at once while accommodating some three hundred or more of their relatives began. This time, the huts had timber walls made from such a hard wood that Schweitzer joked that the termites would need dental treatment. The roofs were made of canvas. Stakes raised

the buildings off the ground. Although Schweitzer's black labor-
ers moved, as he said, only *lento, moderato,* or *adagio,* by the end
of January 1927 a hospital of forty substantial buildings was
complete, though Schweitzer still wished to extend the complex
by providing isolation wards for patients with infectious diseases and creating a special wing for lepers.

He found the new spot preferable to Andende partly
because, in spite of his rule that patients ought whenever possible to be fed by their relatives, he had to give them rice imported
from Europe. Steamships could bring this rice up the river as far
as Lambaréné even when the waters were low. Second, here he
could dig a well, for otherwise his patients infallibly would contract dysentery and compound their other maladies. Third,
unlike Andende, the new site was not set beside a swamp, and
the dangers of malaria thus were lessened considerably. Finally,
there was space: space to keep the doctors' quarters far enough
away from the wards, the smells, and the noise of the patients;
space, if necessary, to enlarge both the staff quarters and the hospital complex; space eventually to build isolation units for
expected epidemics; space for buildings to cater for patients with
contagious diseases.

"As night fell," Schweitzer wrote, "Dr. Lauterbourg and I
made the last journey [from Andende to Adoninalongo], bringing the final patients, among them the mentally ill." Friendly
Europeans helped with the motorboats, one of which was a present to Schweitzer from a Swedish woman, and the paraphernalia
of the hospital was carried upstream in big dugout canoes. The
patients sat quietly and expectantly, for they had been told that
the damp earth of their former hospital was to be replaced with
floors covered with wooden boards. "To them it was as if they
were about to live in a palace," wrote Schweitzer. "I shall never
forget that first evening in the new hospital," he continued.
"From every mosquito-net peered out a happy face." For the first
time, he admitted, his patients were housed as elementary
humanity demanded. And he added one of his increasingly
shrewd appeals: "How thankful I was, thinking of those friends
in Europe through whose generosity I was enabled to face the

cost of removing." He still planned to tear down what remained of his old hospital, using most of the materials to build a new home for his nurses.

In spite of the increasing adulation Schweitzer received, he was under no illusions that his work was the be-all and end-all of missionary hospitals, though he recognized that for governments such tasks were far from their major concerns. They could not dispense with the help of voluntary workers, and Schweitzer said so publicly. In the *Revue des Deux Mondes* of September 1931, he wrote an article on medical help for the colonies. "Let us take note," he said, "that the government, with all the resources at its disposal, will never be in a position to accomplish this task by itself." He marveled at the disproportion between the thousands of square kilometers of French Equatorial Africa, the vast number of the inhabitants, and the few dozen doctors serving the region.

This, he said, lay behind his own initiative in founding in 1913 his tiny hospital in Gabon. Since then, he reported, it had become a fairly considerable enterprise, with three or four doctors and between six and eight European nurses. Many might suppose that their patients, "children of nature, living in the open air underneath a radiant sun, would live far better than those prisoners of offices and factories." The reality was quite other, Schweitzer insisted. In the region of Gabon where he lived, a sexagenarian was a rarity.

Schweitzer recognized that few doctors would wish to devote their entire careers to working in the colonies. He suggested that a good number of young doctors, before establishing themselves in Europe, had several years which they might put at the disposal of Africans, so long as there were organizations that would send them there and furnish them with the means of practicing their vocation.

His attitude toward women workers was fascinatingly realistic. A good number of reasonably well-off women, though qualified and willing to work in hospitals, desired neither the constraints of life in a European clinic nor to take the place of their fellow women who really needed such work. Schweitzer promised that "these independent and enterprising spirits will find the situation of their dreams in a colonial hospital." His own problem was not finding enough volunteers, but paying them.

Schweitzer confessed to his shame an initial antifeminism: He had been unwilling to believe that a woman doctor could keep order among his black male nurses and among the undisciplined "primitives" who peopled his hospital. He had been forced to change his mind. "Lady doctors working in my hospital are even more dominant over the blacks than the other doctors of the stronger sex." Charmed by these women, the blacks served them simply to prove their devotion. That, at least, was the case with the two women doctors working at that moment in Schweitzer's jungle hospital, he said. As if to punish him for his former prejudices, whenever he gave an order to a male nurse, the reply came, "*Oui, doctoresse.*"

He believed that the bare minimum of workers for such a hospital consisted of a carpenter, two nurses, and a doctor. His carpenter, he hoped, would also be able to work in iron as well as wood. The duties he prescribed for his nurses went far beyond what was expected in European hospitals, for while one nurse was looking after the sick and supervising some black nurses, the other would be occupied with housekeeping, in the kitchen, and in the garden and plantation. Schweitzer's attraction to women slyly peeps through his article at this point, for he speedily adds that a colonial hospital can readily employ women who have not qualified as nurses. Laundry, looking after the chickens and goats, cooking, and working in the garden and the plantation are tasks vital for the proper functioning of the hospital, even though they may not seem precisely medical work.

"I am clear that women possessing a general culture are more apt to serve in a colonial hospital than those without this culture," he declared. "They accommodate themselves better to the vicissitudes of colonial life, and accept more easily whatever task is necessary." For this reason, Schweitzer was delighted to welcome such helpers as the exotic wife of the filmmaker Otto

Preminger, who clad herself mostly in chiffon and thus (according to the amused observation of Schweitzer's suave, charmingly wordly-wise Dutch nurse Tony van Leer) usually appeared more naked than the natives themselves.

In contrast to many a contemporary European hospital, the nurses, by Schweitzer's own wish, were also usually quite as cultivated, as intelligent, and as well educated as the doctors. Thus the tight European society over which he presided in French Equatorial Africa formed a homogenous group. Aware of the way his own body and that of Hélène had been abused in their earliest years in Gabon, Schweitzer insisted that after every two years abroad his staff should spend at least six months back in Europe. Again, he hoped that some of his staff would be able to pay for these holidays out of their own pockets, but if this proved impossible, then he begged his European patrons once more to ante up.

As for the assistant doctor, it was vital to find one with a knowledge of surgery. And once a missionary hospital was established, the personnel inevitably must be augmented, rising to two doctors and three nurses. Now one of the doctors could be deployed in visiting the neighboring villages, but on no account could the hospital itself ever be left without a doctor on duty. "When the natives reach the hospital, often tired and suffering privations, for they may well have spent several days journeying for a consultation here, it is vital that they have the certainty of finding a doctor the moment they arrive," Schweitzer insisted. "Otherwise, with the tendency to exaggeration natural amongst the natives, the hospital will speedily acquire an unfortunate reputation which will prevent it from fulfilling the tasks for which it was set up."

Entranced by such a literary wooing, doctors, nurses, and voluntary workers lined up in increasing numbers to serve in Schweitzer's hospital at Lambaréné. Dr. Nessmann returned to Europe, to be replaced by Dr. Frédéric Trenz of Strasbourg. In March 1927, he in turn was replaced by Dr. Mundler. Contingencies of nurses and doctors poured out from Britain and Switzerland. Schweitzer took care that the newspapers took note of their movements, and the newspapers were now ready to oblige him. On the last day of March 1927, *The Times* noted that "Dr. Frances Margaret Harper is to be the second British member of the staff of Dr. Albert Schweitzer's Hospital at Lambaréné, French Gabon (Equatorial Africa). She will leave at the beginning of next week."

In the same year, another report in *The Times* was tantalizingly coy, announcing that a party was leaving from Bordeaux to Lambaréné, consisting of a Swiss doctor, an Alsatian nurse, and (as a voluntary helper) the widow of an English civil servant who was prominently associated with social work. She did not wish to give her name, added *The Times*, though "her Colonial experiences both before and since her marriage have fitted her for the strenuous part of a general helper in hospital work." She was, in fact, Mrs. C. E. B. Russell, as happy to work in the plantation as she was to translate Schweitzer's lectures into English.

CHAPTER 9

◆

A Prophet Honored
and Reviled

After reading *The Quest of the Historical Jesus*, the scholar Theodore Reinach asked Schweitzer, "Are you related to the Schweitzer who wrote the book about Bach," adding, "My wife pretends that you wrote that other book, but that could only be a joke."

As he grew famous, Schweitzer's multifarious personality increasingly stunned his contemporaries. "Albert Schweitzer is one of the most challenging figures in the world today," judged *The Times*, reviewing his *Out of My Life and Thought* in 1931. The reviewer continued: "First because in an age of specialists he is an encyclopaedist, and one who weaves all into a pattern; and then because when he had made himself a master in three, if not four, of the most technical disciplines of modern study, he turned his back on Europe, the fine flower of whose civilization he had culled, in order to devote himself to healing natives in a remote district of the Congo."

The Times set out the enigma in a series of questions. "Was the flight the fruit of disillusion or of faith? Was it the pining of the academic for visible results? Was it restlessness or a great benevolence?" Did Albert Schweitzer himself know? In 1946, one of his correspondents, the Reverend Dr. A. O'Brien of the University of Notre Dame in Indiana included Schweitzer in a monograpoh entitled *Fools for God.* Schweitzer was delighted at the thought. He told O'Brien the story of how, in despair at the way his patients could never be found docilely sitting in the hospital waiting room, he had once exclaimed "What an imbecile I am to have come to stay with these savages and devoted myself to them!" at which, his black assistant Joseph had replied, "Yes, doctor, on earth you are a fool, but not in heaven...."

Schweitzer himself rarely had time for such introspection, continually pressed as he was to keep his hospital financially viable by the profits from his books and from his incessant lecture tours and organ recitals. In January 1926 the situation was already becoming desperate, and Schweitzer issued an open letter of appeal. "In the districts around Lambaréné people are already dying of famine," he reported. "I have still enough rice for about a fortnight for the hospital. If I do not get further supplies I do not know how I shall feed my patients. It is terrible to see the famine. Rice has doubled in price in three months, and I must have 60 kilos a day, if not more."

Regular bulletins now were issued from the hospital to keep his friends and well-wishers informed of the needs and happenings of the jungle hospital. One contained more information about the problem: "Since July the import of rice from Europe and India on which we depend here has been quite insufficient," wrote Schweitzer. "Three thousand tons were spoilt by sea water in a leaking boat. The deficit has not yet been made good. I was able to procure two tons of rice in July, and I have collected another by rushing about in my motor boat. I gave the mission in Samkita 160 kilogrammes of rice, as they had come to the end of their supplies. I also gave 100 kilogrammes to a large English factory for the native workmen; they had nothing at all."

Yet Schweitzer knew how to end his bulletins and letters on a hopeful note. "In about seven weeks the bananas which were planted last year will bear fruit," said the bulletin. And his letter ended, "Nevertheless, despite these cares, I am profoundly happy in my work." The personal details too were appealing. The African patients were to him both a joy and a constant irritation. "They take my planks and use them for their fires, and they take and break everything that can be taken or broken." They had no idea of order, so that when you wanted to give them medicine you had to go and find them. "But you cannot be severe with them," he continued, "for usually they reach me mere living skeletons and with terrible sores on their feet." Thus Schweitzer painted a picture of his toils, and countless people responded generously. It was hard to resist helping a man who was evidently wearing himself out in his cause. Mrs. C. E. B. Russell had gone out with the intention of teaching Schweitzer English. He never fully mastered it: "I have been so tired that for a long time I have had again to abandon my studies in English."

Schweitzer was hard-pressed to find time for his philosophy. On September 12, 1928, he even delegated Hélène to write on his behalf to his friend Oskar Kraus: "My husband is so busy and so tired that he has asked me to thank you heartily in his place for your delightful letter." Five years later, on December 10, 1933, we find Schweitzer in the same state. "I am writing no letters," he tells Kraus. "All my 'free time' (it is so little!) is devoted to philosophy."

"Your energy is wonderful," wrote Nathan Söderblom on December 30, 1932. Once again, Schweitzer was back in Europe, giving lectures and concerts in Britain, Sweden, Holland, Switzerland, and Germany, as well as collecting honorary degrees. His chief engagement had been to deliver in the opera house of Frankfurt am Main the memorial address on the centenary of Goethe's death. It is a measure of Schweitzer's remarkable stature that, oddly enough, he was no Goethe expert. Of the eighty-five books on Goethe in his library at Gunsbach, only six are annotated, a sure sign that he had not read the rest. To his great surprise, Schweitzer had been awarded the Goethe Prize by the same city in 1928, the second person to be given it after Stefan George. His address of thanks that year—apart from a lecture on *Faust* that he gave in Paris in 1899 and a few scattered references in his edition of Bach—was virtually the first reference to Goethe in his entire published works. He spent the money buying a home in Gunsbach, which he initially planned as a rest center for his hospital personnel during their holidays.

On March 22, 1932, at the exact hour of Goethe's death one hundred years previously, Schweitzer began his speech. It was filled with gloom. "We are remembering the death of Goethe in the most stupendous hour of fate that ever sounded for humanity." Schweitzer deplored the political developments that were consuming the German nation, regarding both panaceas of communism and National Socialism as "economic and social witchcraft," which forced the individual to surrender his material and spiritual independence. Goethe was of enormous significance for the age precisely because he had nothing in common with it. His message, said Schweitzer, was that men and women must not abandon the ideal of personal, individual humanity, "even when this seems no longer tenable beside the opportunistic theories which aim at subordinating the spiritual to the material."

By the time Schweitzer returned to Lambaréné, the Nazis had come to power in Germany. With their Jewish heritage, Hélène and Rhena, increasingly estranged from Albert Schweitzer, had fled to safety in Switzerland. The following year, Schweitzer returned to spend two more years in Europe as Hibbert lecturer at Manchester College, Oxford, and as Gifford lecturer in Edinburgh. These lectures, and one he gave at London University, were variations on his current wrestling with the problems of religion and modern civilization. He combined them, as usual, with organ recitals. The one change in his routine was his refusal to enter Nazi Germany. Six months was all he could spare for Lambaréné in 1935, for he was obliged to return to Europe in September to deliver the second course of his Gifford lectures.

On his sixtieth birthday, Schweitzer was delighted to have a park in Strasbourg named after him. He was less pleased with a letter from Hitler's minister of propaganda, Dr. Goebbels, which ended "With German greetings." Schweitzer delicately insulted Goebbels by ending his reply, "With Central African greetings."

Then for nearly two years, from February 1937 to January 1939, Schweitzer remained at Lambaréné, again without his wife.

The Second World War forced them together. Albert arrived in Europe at the beginning of 1939 and immediately decided that war was imminent. His immediate thoughts were to provide for his hospital. For ten days he was in Alsace, gathering together drugs and equipment. He briefly met Hélène and Rhena, who had become engaged to a French organ builder named Jean Eckert. Then he returned to his jungle hospital. The staff was depleted, with only one doctor besides Schweitzer and only four European nurses. For this reason, and because he feared that the imminent war would last a long time, Schweitzer was obliged to send many patients home.

When war did break out, most of the French African colonies declared for General de Gaulle and in opposition to Hitler. Only Gabon faltered. In consequence, Free French troops loyal to de Gaulle invaded. During the fighting, which lasted from October 13 to November 5, Schweitzer's hospital was declared neutral territory. Fortunately, the doctor and his staff took the precaution of barricading the place, for occasionally the troops came within rifle shot of the buildings and bullets screamed through the once peaceful grounds.

Albert had taken advantage of the slump in trade to buy cheap timber and expand his hospital, once again laboring himself alongside his African workers during the building program. He bought a massive amount of rice cheaply because it was infested with weevils, and everyone ate it. Once the Free French had liberated Lambaréné, supplies could sail, however fitfully, from Britain and the United States. Much of the credit for the generosity of the Americans must go to Hélène Schweitzer. The year before World War II broke out, she and Rhena set off without Albert on a fund-raising tour of the United States, lecturing about the work at Lambaréné. In spite of Albert's heroic efforts, supplies at the hospital were beginning to run out by the time Hélène and Rhena's work in the United States began to pay off, and generous Americans started sending medicines and funds across the Atlantic. The first consignment of drugs, surgical instruments, and kitchenware arrived in May 1942.

Hélène herself had by now reached Lambaréné. Her previous lodgings with Rhena and Jean in Paris became dangerous once the Nazis took over the city. Describing herself as the most senior nurse of Lambaréné, she managed to obtain a British visa from the Red Cross society in Geneva, and when the Nazis took over Paris the three of them set off by car for Bordeaux. Hélène went on to neutral Portugal and in a Portuguese steamer sailed to Angola. Doggedly, she continued by car as far as the Ogowe, and on August 2, 1941, she arrived at her husband's jungle hospital. Throughout the war she toiled there as a nurse, her ailments apparently forgotten.

Albert feared that he was wearing himself out. As he put it in a Lambaréné bulletin of 1944, he longed for a single free day when he might sleep enough to rid himself of his increasing fatigue. He longed to concentrate on his writing, to study his music, and to play the organ, indeed, simply "to walk, to dream, to read simply for the sake of refreshment." Would that day ever come? he wondered.

Americans increasingly became Schweitzer's chief financial resource, and an American Albert Schweitzer Fellowship soon numbered thousands in its membership. In 1947, two American Unitarians, Charles R. Joy and Melvin Arnold, came to Lambaréné to present the doctor with a check for more than four thousand dollars. Melvin Arnold was editor-in-chief of the Boston Unitarian publishing house, The Beacon Press, and he was determined to make Schweitzer's writings better known in the United States. In consequence, attractively presented books such as *The Animal World of Albert Schweitzer: Jungle Insights into Reverence for Life*, a work translated and edited by Charles R. Joy, soon appeared, meeting with such demand that the book was reprinted frequently. In the meantime, a special issue of the Boston Unitarian journal *The Christian Register* had been devoted to Schweitzer, and a Roman Catholic priest, Father John O'Brien, had described Schweitzer in *The Reader's Digest* as "the greatest soul in Christendom." In October 1947, *Life* magazine went even further with an article titled, "The Greatest Man in the World—

That Is What Some People Call Albert Schweitzer, Jungle Philosopher."

Inevitably, Schweitzer was drawn to visit the United States. Initially he refused. Princeton offered him the chance to write away from turmoil. His hospital, as he told Albert Einstein, made him "no longer a free man." The Americans persisted, and repeatedly Schweitzer refused their invitations. Then, in 1949, Walter Paepke, founder of the Institute for Humanistic Studies at Aspen, Colorado, asked Schweitzer to come and lecture there. His fee would be five thousand dollars. Once more Schweitzer refused. He changed his mind when Paepke promised to pay the fee in French francs and asked him to speak about Goethe on the bicentenary of the poet's birth.

Schweitzer was still far from a Goethe expert. In a letter to Charles R. Joy, who translated his five Goethe studies for The Beacon Press, he confessed, "I cannot tell exactly the extent and the intensity of Goethe's influence upon me. It is impossible to determine in what he has influenced me and in what he had only confirmed me in the way I was already taking." Schweitzer concluded, "I believe that the latter rather than the former is the more important," adding, "As for the idea of reverence for life, I think I am right in saying that he had no part in the genesis of the idea or of the words."

Where he felt akin to Goethe was that in both of them the active life had greatly impinged upon their intellectual lives. "Both of us have this in common: our lives have so developed that the activities we have undertaken have not permitted us to bring our intellectual lifework to an end in composure and leisure," he told Joy. "Only by virtue of enormous exertions have we finished a goodly fragment of it."

Nonetheless, he blithely went to Aspen and lectured on his newly found fellow activist. He went so far as to assert that Goethe's greatness was, so to speak, akin to his own, by reason of the many sides of his predecessor's character. Why had Goethe gradually acquired a choice place among the great poets of the world? "Because this great poet is at the same time a great master of natural science, a great thinker, a great man." Goethe's very imagery proclaimed him a visionary, said Schweitzer. Goethe took Faustian risks and overcame them. And yet he was also a man of common sense. Schweitzer quoted one of the aphorisms of Goethe's old age: "I have always been wary of philosophy. My point of view had always been that of common sense."

Goethe had turned his incessantly active life into a virtue (as had Schweitzer, in spite of his continual laments). In the Aspen lecture, Schweitzer observed how in *Faust* the poet had taken liberties with the first verse of the Gospel of Saint John, altering "In the beginning was the Word" to read "In the beginning was the action." Schweitzer complied. "By action a man finds it easiest to come to terms with himself." As Goethe had insisted that one should simply perform what the day demands, so, said Schweitzer, we open our eyes to assess our immediate tasks, and we take them up.

As for Goethe's pantheism, Schweitzer was able to take it in his stride. At least it was far from arid dogmatism. He discovered in Goethe's notion of a God speaking deep in his own being a similar mysticism to his own. He also seems to hint at another similarity between Goethe's relations with Christiane Vulpius and his own with Hélène (who had accompanied him to America). When he came to consider Goethe's possible faults, Schweitzer began by observing that he did not understand how the poet could have lived with Christiane for eighteen months before legalizing the situation and giving her the proper status for the role she already was playing. "How could he so prolong a state of affairs which brought him and especially her so many difficulties and so many humiliations?" He asked too why Goethe was so often cold in the presence of other people's griefs, and why at times he could behave so unnaturally.

As Schweitzer observed, Goethe's life embraced many contradictions. But among the fundamental traits of his character was a passion for truth. Intrigue was completely alien to his nature. A man of immense gifts, he was nonetheless humble both before God and before his fellow human beings. Generous, he longed to serve. "This is Goethe, the poet, the savant, the thinker and the man to whom our thoughts are particularly devoted at this moment. And among us here and others far off there are those who, thinking of him, have thanked him for what he had given them: his ethical and religious wisdom, so simple and so profound," his lecture concluded. "I acknowledge myself as one of their number."

Among his audience were some of the world's most renowned philosphers, musicians, theologians, historians, and writers. They included Martin Buber and Artur Rubinstein. Schweitzer delivered the lecture twice, the first time in French, when his translator was Emory Ross (head of the Albert Schweitzer Fellowship), the second time in German, when his translator was Thornton Wilder. After Aspen, Schweitzer visited Chicago to receive an honorary degree from the university and star at a luncheon and reception among whose seventeen hundred guests was Governor Adlai Stevenson. Schweitzer also took care to visit the pharmaceutical factory in New York that had sent him so many drugs. Amid the adulation, he did not lose his sense of humor. On a railway train in the Midwest two ladies, mistaking him for Albert Einstein, whose own hair and mustache were almost as disheveled as Schweitzer's, asked for his autograph. Schweitzer signed, "Albert Einstein, by way of his friend Albert Schweitzer."

He and Hélène returned first to Europe and then to Lambaréné. In July 1950, Hélène, her physical ailments once more oppressive, felt the need to return to Europe. Albert took her to Port-Gentil, and as they left Lambaréné he could not help thinking that she probably would never return. He returned to his hospital and devoted himself both to his patients and to his nurses and doctors.

For one of them he even wrote a book. Dr. Anna Wildikann needed a car for her future work in Israel. To earn the money, Schweitzer wrote one of the most charming tales of this century, *The Story of My Pelican*. The hero of this book happens to be not the pelican, but its master and savior Albert Schweitzer. In the beginning, in a nest above the river, the little pelican and his two brothers are startled when some black men drive away their parents and carry off the three of them, their feet bound together. They reach a spot with palm trees and mangoes and red-roofed buildings. Dogs snap at them, and then a powerful voice stills the noise. A burly man appears, accompanied by a woman in white. "I later discovered," says the pelican, "that they were Dr. Schweitzer and the nurse Emma Hausknecht."

Schweitzer buys the three pelicans. The lady doctor, Anna Wildikann, adores their downy rumps and tries to stroke them. The doctor builds them a little hutch. Eventually the little pelican's brothers fly off, but not this one. "Let us hope the little one will follow their example," says Schweitzer. Says the pelican, "I swore that the doctor would not be rid of me so easily. I know better than he does what is good for me." Occasionally, lady pelicans ask him to leave the hospital and set up home with them in a faraway tree. "But," says the pelican, "I have always stuck to the hospital grounds, and I plan to go on sticking to them."

Schweitzer's charming tale reveals an insight into his own often curmudgeonly self. "He was busy all afternoon under the houses, crawling around and making not the slightest attempt to hide the bad temper these extraordinary activities put him in," notes the pelican. "I have never had any experience of human beings, and I found it very odd that such a good man could grumble so often."

The story was based on Schweitzer's favorite pelican, a bird he named Parsifal, whom some Africans had brought to the hospital. Yet for all its sweetness, the tale he wrote about the bird betrays no sentimentality in the man who preached reverence for life. Eventually, someone peppered the real Parsifal with shotgun pellets. One of his doctors, Frank Catchpool, noticing that the bird had made a particularly clumsy crash landing at the pharmacy, wanted to treat Parsifal before Schweitzer's human patients. Schweitzer would not allow this. "No, leave the pelican alone," he ordered. "I don't want you to waste your time. I don't want you to waste the materials of the hospital on this. I'll look after my pelican." Schweitzer put the bird outside his window. After four or five days he noticed that it still was not eating. He asked Catchpool for a diagnosis, which was that the bird was dehydrating and would surely die. "If he's not better tomor-row," responded Schweitzer, "I'll chop his head off." The reply pleased Dr. Catchpool, for it revealed that Schweitzer would never allow sentiment to overrule his reason.

Honors continued to flow thick and fast. In 1950 Schweitzer accepted the French offer to become a chevalier of the Legion of Honor, having turned down this honor the first time around as a bitter reprisal for all he and Hélène had suffered at the hands of the French during World War I. In 1951, he was elected a mem-ber of the French Academy of Moral and Political Sciences. In 1952, King Gustav Adolf of Sweden awarded him the Prince Charles Medal in recognition of his humanitarian achievements. The following year he received from Queen Elizabeth II of Britain the Order of Merit, thus becoming the only non-Briton ever to be given this honor, apart from Dwight D. Eisenhower, who as supreme commander of the Allied forces, had just led the free world to victory over Hitler.

As the world struggled to pull itself up out of the horrors of the most devastating war of all time, Queen Elizabeth was thus honoring in Eisenhower the great warrior and in Schweitzer the great healer. Small wonder that these two men now came in near the top of every popularity poll in the United States, the United Kingdom, and the continent of Europe. The Schweitzer phe-nomenon was now more than mere celebrity or even mere fame. A near mania had swept parts of America during his visit. Now, in Britain, hundreds of people, including such luminaries as Bertrand Russell and the composer Vaughan Williams, thronged to meet him, many inching slowly forward to shake his hand as he sat in the restaurant his Alsatian friend Emil Mettler had set up in Petty France, London.

Yet Schweitzer remained a shy person. Perhaps he also wished to retain control over his own myth. In 1947, while he was resolutely dissuading an American film company from com-ing to Lambaréné, he wrote to Professor Everett Skillings of Mid-dlebury College, Vermont, "I recounted both my life and my work in my autobiography. That is the authentic film." On February 14, 1951, he firmly refused to allow Gilbert Cesbron, author of the celebrated play *It Is Midnight, Dr. Schweitzer*, to come to film in Lambaréné. "I can allow only simple documentaries to be made of the daily life of the hospital," he insisted. "All I want is authenticity, absolute authenticity. I believe it is my historian's soul which dictates this attitude. If I have managed to achieve several things in history (discovered some secrets of the life of Jesus and the thinking of St. Paul) it is because I am always seeking absolute authenticity." On August 13, 1954, he was threatening legal action to stop a proposed Hollywood movie about him, scripted by Irving Wallace.

One who did manage to shoot a film was his close friend, the American Erica Anderson. She too had been refused permission, but he invited her to visit Lambaréné provided she respected his wishes. Erica Anderson arrived with her camera and an assistant solely because she had been commissioned by an art collector to film for him in the Congo. As her friendship with Schweitzer grew, he relented. She could film him and his hospital, but on condition that no one else would be told about this concession and that the film would be shown only after his death. It includes a fascinating pictorial revelation of the doctor's reticence. Schweitzer looks at the camera hesitantly, almost distrustfully, and he speaks quietly and equally hesitantly.

Even in his eightieth year this reticence was still to the fore. When the Reverend Richard E. Evans of the World Parliament of Religions wrote asking if he could bring out a party of well-wishers to celebrate Schweitzer's eightieth birthday at Lambaréné, Schweitzer telegraphed "NO" from Gunsbach. In a following letter he explained that he suffered from being famous. "I am afraid of the great honour which you bestow on me publically, in the view of all the world. And your visit would do this in a strong measure. For that reason please do let me be as I am, someone who lives and works in silence."

And yet he was a tireless correspondent. Night after night he toiled at his letters. "My hand, gnawed at with writer's cramp, is causing me some grief (and almost refuses to serve me any more)," he told Monsieur Jean Mozul on October 22, 1945. "I cannot write to you as I should like." But he never stopped writing these nighttime letters. On May 5, 1951, he confessed to Dr. H. van Lunzen of Odoorn, Holland, that, "My correspondence is in chaos, for in the midst of my work, and tired as I am, I cannot even finish the business correspondence for the hospital. All letters have to be written at night, in hours which I so much need for sleep."

In spite of his many years in Africa, to work in the hot and moist climate of Africa was still at times almost impossible for him. "Here in the low parts of the virgin forest it is worst," he told his Unitarian friend Charles Joy in a letter of January 23, 1945. "Farther in the interior, in regions of some more altitude, it is better." He continued, "I have the splendid privilege, for which I thank God every day, that I can stand this climate fairly well, but some of my co-workers suffer much from it. One of our nurses has been so exhausted by it, that she had to be sent back to the Cameroons in August 1944 to restore her health and is recovering only very slowly." But the climate still took its toll.

Still, Lambaréné was dear to Schweitzer's heart, and his affection for his jungle home shines through his correspondence. He described the spot to Sister Jacopa Sorella on August 14, 1962: "I am writing to you in the evening by the light of a petrol lamp. We have no electricity in our rooms. The petrol lamp is more intimate. On my table three cats are sleeping, one big one and two little ones. They love the gentle warmth of the lamp. In the large village which is our hospital we have many animals. They live in peace together." Schweitzer was writing to thank Sister Sorella for her gifts, for this incessant correspondence was undoubtedly part of his ceaseless efforts to raise funds for Lambaréné.

Schweitzer was as firm about publishing his letters as he was about being filmed. In 1956 the Catholic historian Daniel Rops wrote asking whether one of his private letters might be published in the revue *Ecclesia*, with a response from a Catholic theologian. Schweitzer replied, "I have a principle to which I remain ever faithful: never to allow a letter of mine to be published if I can prevent it." He continued, "For me a letter is something entirely personal, an improvisation, a communication with another personality. Publication addresses the multitude. It is objective, written in measured and carefully chosen terms." So, Schweitzer said, let us both try to explore, in our intimate friendship, our beliefs so as to come to understand different traditions. He ended his letter by looking forward to a private discussion with Rops when he was next in Paris, adding, "I am writing to you late in the night, after a most tiring day."

Writing to his friend Fritz Buri in 1950, he issued the same order. "Beware. This letter is for your eyes only," he insisted. "You must read no part of it to any other person. You must not copy out any of it for anyone. Do not try to get around my veto."

Some of his deepest admirers failed to obey his rule, and Schweitzer himself was the one to suffer for it. George Marshall, a friend of Charles Joy and Melvin Arnold, was minister of a Unitarian church in Boston, and in 1961 he invited Schweitzer to become a member. Schweitzer replied, "I heartfully thank you for your offer to make me an honorary member of the Unitarian church. I accept with pleasure." George Marshall gleefully published the letter in his next news bulletin. The subsequent furor inevitably suggested that Schweitzer, the onetime heretic, had finally abandoned orthodox Christianity. Schweitzer was obliged to deny the charge in an interview in *Time* magazine, stating that "there is no question of my breaking with the Lutheran Church." He was, he declared, a Protestant and, above all, a scientist, as such "on good terms with all Protestant Churches."

But he refused to justify himself further. As he wrote to George Marshall, "I have no intention of explaining to people why I also remain a member of the Unitarian church. If they don't understand what the Unitarian church stands for, they can take up an encyclopedia and instruct themselves."

At the heart of his questioning and his respect for other religions, Schweitzer had in truth retained a firm, even straightforward Christian faith. His demeanor, like his writings, concealed a pietistic and gentle heart. "In August John's admirable drawing of him Dr. Schweitzer looks slightly unkempt and fierce," wrote Nathaniel Micklem. "No one could possibly be less fierce than he! We found him the most unassuming and brotherly of men. After some long discussion of his view upon the Gospels I once asked him in what sort of form he would express his faith. The Lord's prayer, he answered, expressed his creed."

What at times misled people into believing that he had abandoned his faith was Schweitzer's subtleties of exposition, combined with his natural reticence. As he told one correspondent, Erwin R. Jacobi, in 1962, he had never believed in a "God-personality directing the world." In a notorious letter of 1924 to Oskar Kraus, he declared, "I never speak of the philosophy of 'God' but of 'the universal will to live.'" In the same year he would write to his close friend Martin Werner that "an unexpressed simple Christianity surrounds my philosophy." In this letter he acknowledged that "many are disturbed that I do not broadcast my relationships to Christianity." He added, "But others, not I, should clarify the relationship of my thoughts to Christianity."

The radical critiques of his *Quest* continued to bemuse some of his admirers, and Schweitzer patiently tried to put them right. When, in 1960, he received a letter expressing such bemusement from a correspondent from Alsace named Alfred Haefels, Schweitzer patiently corrected him. "You can calm yourself. I am not the one who has claimed that the existence of Jesus is a myth. On the contrary: it is I who combatted that opinion. Certain German and American historians formulated it towards 1900 and later." Schweitzer added the breathtaking claim that anyone who read his work *The Quest of the Historical Jesus* would find such notions completely refuted.

In 1953 Schweitzer's benevolence was betrayed viciously by the British journalist James Cameron. Initially, Cameron came to Lambaréné to interview "the only man in this century who had become famous by being good." His aim was to write some pieces about Schweitzer for the London *News Chronicle* and also to broadcast about him on the BBC. Schweitzer charmed Cameron with his prodigious wink, his jokes (informing a dog that chased his chickens that this was a Peace Prize home), and his gift of friendship. "I often forgot in the mornings that Albert

Schweitzer was The World's Finest Man," Cameron told the readers of the *News Chronicle;* "I felt him merely to be one of the friendliest."

But then the hard-bitten journalist took over. "I would say that the hospital today exists for him rather than he for it," judged Cameron. "Here it is: deliberately archaic and primitive, deliberately part of the jungle around it, a background of his own creation which probably means a good deal more philosophically than it does medically."

Cameron had married an Indian woman and probably was ultrasensitive to what he supposed were slights to Schweitzer's black assistants. He disliked the way the doctor pummeled them to work. "Run, you! Work like a white man, can't you!" Schweitzer roared. Even Cameron was forced to admit that the Africans moved so slowly that one could scarcely spot it. "It was like watching a slow motion film!" he wrote. "Sometimes work slowed down to a point where movement, if it existed, was imperceptible; it was like studying the hour-hand of a watch."

In 1967 James Cameron set out his resentment of Schweitzer in a section of his autobiography, *Point of Departure.* He began with the remark that Lambaréné fulfilled the doctor's insistence on remoteness and self-containment, and also his resistance to progress, as if Schweitzer's care for the black peoples could have expressed itself somewhere closer to Cameron's civilized Fleet Street society. In this book Cameron boasted of being the first to challenge the legend of Schweitzer, the first heretic. When he first met Schweitzer, he already was resisting his warmth. "He was big; I had not previously thought of him as so tall; a heavy man in crumpled drill trousers and a short sleeved shirt, and the rest according to the legend—the bush of disordered hair, the undergrowth of moustache, the aggressive nose, the eyes of an old man," Cameron remembered. "He hurried across the room to greet me with such momentary enthusiasm I felt he must be mistaking me for somebody else; but he was impatient for dinner."

After dinner Schweitzer left the table, crossed the room, and played a cracked chord on the ancient piano. Everyone sang *"Reste avec moi, Seigneur, le jour décline."* Then the company said the Lord's Prayer amid the hiss and rumble of the rain. The following morning Cameron saw the doctor through his mosquito net, shuffling up the path to the leper village, sheltering from the rain under a huge umbrella. Then the sun that Schweitzer had endured for forty years beat down. And next Cameron saw the hospital.

"I had been prepared for some professional unorthodoxies, but not this glaring squalor," he reported. "The wards were rude huts, airless and dark, plank beds and wooden pillows; every one infested with hens and dogs." Dimly, Cameron noted that in Gabon, which was ruled by fetishism and superstition, the primitive African would not go to the hospital at all if he could help it: "He was obliged to bring his wives and their children, his goats and his poultry, in a comfortable congestion of brown flesh and feathers." Yet this insight disappeared in his desire to indict Albert Schweitzer. "The Doctor had fenced off all mechanical advances to a degree that seemed both pedantic and appalling," said Cameron.

Insufficiently acquainted with Schweitzer's philosophy of reverence for life, Cameron next assayed a meager criticism of Schweitzer's behavior. "One day in the plantation he suddenly pulled me aside; a column of soldier ants was crossing the track; it seemed they had the right of way. During the rains these creatures can be formidable; they can march half a dozen abreast in precise military order, and can be menacing to any small creature that falls in the path of their advance. Nevertheless, this multiplicity of life had to be protected from footfall. A little later, however, the Doctor stopped to gather a handful of fallen palmnuts for Tekla, his wild pig; he did not observe that the orange nuts were crawling with ants until they began to bite him. It was a pleasure to see how smartly and with what vigour the Doctor knocked them flying, without regard to their finer feelings." Small wonder that Cameron was disturbed when Schweitzer cleaned his boots on the tufts of Tekla's back.

Someone had told Cameron that Schweitzer had behaved badly to his wife and daughter. His article and book transformed this rumor into the statement that he had imposed on them a cruel loneliness, which "contrasted with his cultivation of the rich dilettante women who affected to nurse at his shrine." No doubt Schweitzer (and his entourage of nurses) indulgently accepted the visits of such entertaining dilettante women as Olga Deterding and Marion Preminger; but the remark slandered the devoted work, in viciously enervating conditions, of many female volunteers who found a deeply satisfying vocation in coming to Lambaréné. They suffered the heat and rain far more than did James Cameron. As one of them, Ali Silver, told me, when she left Gabon she was glad at last to throw her topee into the Ogowe.

James Cameron in his time passed as a distinguished journalist. In reality, he was a disgrace to his profession. Schweitzer himself spotted it, murmuring to Cameron, "Yours must be a distressing occupation; rather useless." Yet Cameron's work undoubtedly harmed the reputation of Albert Schweitzer. And there is a damaging discrepancy between Cameron's memories of their meetings and what he chose to represent as the truth in *Point of Departure*. Their talk had turned to Daniel F. Malan, the nationalist leader of white South Africa whose political program involved moving the blacks of his nation to separate territories, entirely segregated from the whites. "Schweitzer argued, and I think with some reason, that Malan was a patriarchal tyrant, rather than a fascist tyrant, the way his successors became," Cameron confessed, when interviewed by the author James Brabazon. "And I think there's something to be said for that." But what Cameron wrote was that the doctor "proposed to me his opinion that the most salutary influence on the African race question had been the late Dr. Malan." He supposedly was recording the opinions of a man married to a converted Jew, an Alsatian who hated the Nazis whom Malan had so much admired.

Can one believe the rest of Cameron's assertions? Schweitzer, he wrote, declared that "he had never in forty years taken an African to his table, and that indeed in no circumstances could he contemplate the possibility of an *indigène* being seated in his presence." A cursory glance at the photographs in the many books about Albert Schweitzer would have spotted blacks happily sitting while the doctor stood.

What turned James Cameron against Albert Schweitzer? Was the doctor's own hard-boiled wit too much for the cynicism of the journalist? Schweitzer had reprimanded Cameron for walking alone up the track that led through the forest and past the settlement, heedless of the danger from gorillas. Fatuously, Cameron responded that by now the neighboring gorillas might have learned respect for life from the great doctor. With acerbity Schweitzer replied, "Doubtless if you communicated to the gorilla that you were a member of the British Press, he would stand aside; if by chance you had no time to do so he would first break your arms, then your legs, one by one: following that he would tear off your scalp." Schweitzer ended this admonition with, "Gorillas I know."

The most damaging part of Cameron's indictment was, of course, his accusation that Schweitzer was a racist. The charge is both hard to sustain and not entirely easy to refute. Schweitzer's attitude to the black races changed during half a century. What remained consistent was his desire to serve them and his recognition that his respect for them seemed initially ridiculous. When in his *Civilisation and Ethics* Schweitzer described his ideal man who lived according to the principles of reverence for life, he added that such a person must expect to be mocked as sentimental. "It is the fate of every truth to be thus ridiculed before it is recognised," he countered, adding, "It was once considered stupid to think that black men were really human. That stupidity has now become a truth."

Schweitzer's writings often reveal, almost en passant, his habitual courtesy to the black people among whom he worked. In the celebrated passage that describes the inspiration for his ethic of reverence for life, he tells us that in September 1915 he had been to visit the sick wife of a missionary at N'Gômô, some two hundred kilometers upstream. The only conveyance he could find was a little steamer towing scows. "Except for myself there were only blacks on board, among them my friend from Lambaréné Emil Ogoumd," he continued. "As in my hurry I had not been able to provide sufficient food, they permitted me to eat with them out of their cooking pot."

From the beginning of his life to its end, he remained convinced that the white races had treated the blacks grievously. "This noble culture of ours!" he exclaimed in the pulpit of Saint-Nicolas, Strasbourg, on the first Sunday of January 1905. "Speaking so piously of human dignity and human rights, it then disregards the dignity and the rights of countless millions, treading them underfoot simply because they live overseas or because their skins are of a different colour, or because they cannot help themselves."

His article in *The Contemporary Review* of January 1928 on "The Relations of the White and Coloured Races" is scathing about the impact of the white man on black people. "The independence of primitive or semi-primitive peoples is lost at the moment when the first white man's boat arrives with powder or rum, salt or fabrics," Schweitzer declared. "The social, economic and political situation at that moment begins to be turned upside down. The chiefs begin to sell their subjects for goods." Westerners must ask themselves, "Have we a right to be here?" Are we here simply as masters of these folk and their lands, simply using them as raw material for our industries? Or have we a duty to create a new social order, so that the native peoples can resist the evil encroachments of white civilization?

The blacks, Schweitzer argued, have seven fundamental rights. They had the right to live where their lives had developed, without being displaced for the sake of modern communications. They had a right to circulate freely, regardless of whether the vast cocoa plantations needed them to stay put as available labor or the white tax authorities found it easier to dun them if they remained in one place. They had a right to the soil, and to develop it as they saw fit. Next, said Schweitzer, they had the right to free work and to free exchange, for often he noticed that Africans were forcibly removed from their own homes to work elsewhere, and (he knew) "the African loses his vitality and his elasticity directly when you take him from his village."

The three remaining rights were to justice; to a natural,

national organization that would ensure "a stable population, possessing houses, fields, orchards, workshops, and the requisite capacity to create and use them;" and to education. Here Schweitzer was at pains to praise the missionary societies, for if he wanted to find, say, a carpenter who could work really skillfully with his hands, he could find none save those educated by missionary societies. "When the modern State talks about doing an educational work among the natives, I say to it: 'Do not make phrases; show me your work. How many educators have you in fact exported to your colony?'"

The essential feeling of any relationship between whites and blacks, Schweitzer insisted in his book *On the Edge of the Primeval Forest*, must be "a real feeling of brotherliness." But then he added the paternalistic words, "The negro is a child, and with children nothing can be done without the use of authority. We must, therefore, so arrange the circumstances of daily life that my natural authority can find expression. With regard to the negroes, then, I have coined the formula: 'I am your brother, it is true, but your elder brother.'"

Schweitzer insisted that "the negro is not idle, but he is a free man; hence he is always a casual worker, with whose labour no regular industry can be carried on." Undoubtedly he was speaking from personal experience. In *More from the Primeval Forest*, which evaluates his second stint in Africa in the mid-1920s, a note of disillusion has crept in. "Had I any say in the matter," he wrote, "no black man would be allowed to read and write without being apprenticed to some trade." The Africans, he asserted, were unable "to assert themselves or adapt to difficult circumstances." As late as 1947, Schweitzer insisted that several generations must elapse before the African blacks would be civilized. Meanwhile, the Africans must be given a "limited freedom" and instructed in the "concept of humanity." These were the views that in 1962 provoked the veteran black activist W. E. B. Du Bois to urge Schweitzer to abandon "mere alms-giving and paternalistic feeding of children from a silver spoon" and instead "train Negroes as assistants and helpers, surround himself with a growing African staff of scientifically educated natives who can in time carry on to spread his work and see that it does not continue to be dependent on European charity." Du Bois added the comment that "the work of men like Dr. Schweitzer in medicine deserves all praise." He conceded that "the missionary of medicine is sorely needed in Africa. But the defenders of manhood are needed even more."

Paternalism also governed Schweitzer's response to the political problems that arose in the Belgian Congo at the beginning of the 1960s. Once the colony had achieved independence, it split in two. The wealthiest part, Katanga, buttressed by its copper mines, seceded from the rest under the leadership of Moise Tshombe. The poorest region, led by a former post office clerk named Patrice Emery Lumumba who was murdered in 1962, hoped to throw the whites out of the Congo, whereas Tshombe, backed by Belgian money, firmly intended to use them.

Schweitzer, who had made a vow not to speak about politics, broke it and unswervingly backed Katanga. Colonization alone was responsible for putting the two states together, he argued. In reality they had nothing in common. What is more, Schweitzer urged, the people ruled by Lumumba were idle, whereas the Katangans were hard-working, diligent, and comparatively well educated.

For expressing these views Schweitzer found himself the butt of anger from the Western world. The Security Council of the United Nations had sent troops to the Congo, hoping to force Moise Tshombe to give away some of his country's wealth to Lumumba's government in Léopoldville. Dag Hammarskjöld, secretary-general of the United Nations, flew out to try to influence the situation and met with his death when his airplane crashed.

If Albert Schweitzer was distressed that some of his most distinguished contemporaries disagreed with his analysis, Bertrand Russell was one of them. On January 15, 1962, he wrote to tell Schweitzer, "In my view, Belgian rule of the Congo was an appalling example of cruel exploitation. No civil service was trained, no education provided, and virtually no medical attention given to the African population. Upon yielding political independence, the Belgians consciously set out to create chaos, death, and disorder in the newly independent State." Russell characterized the question thus: "The issue in Katanga is whether the great wealth should go to European Cartels while Africans starve in the Congo or whether the wealth of the country should be administered by an African Government centrally to develop schools, roads, hospitals, housing—the essentials of a modern society."

Schweitzer did not deign to reply until Russell wrote again, reiterating the same points. Then, in unaccustomed English, Schweitzer politely told the British philosopher that he did not know what he was talking about. "The Congo state is in a bad situation, because the Congo government was unable to bring order and put people to work," he pointed out. The Katanga state, he asserted, is a state with a good government, in which peace prevails and where people work. In another letter to Russell, Schweitzer declared that the United Nations had behaved "with an incredible lightheartedness and an unpardonable brutality." Brutally enough, he told his English friend, "Please, kindly excuse, that I cannot fully agree with you, because I know the facts."

But his letter characteristically carried an olive branch. He wrote that "in all other matters concerning world politics do we go hand in hand. And now do we know, that also have come to nothing the negotiations for abolishment of nuclear explosions." The atheist Russell was not the only world figure Schweitzer was now associated with in an attempt to outlaw the atomic bomb. Pastor Martin Niemöller, the former German U-boat commander and opponent of Adolf Hitler, now became his ally. (Niemöller discovered to his horror that during World War I he had almost sunk with a torpedo a ship carrying Schweitzer.) So did Schweitzer's cousin Jean-Paul Sartre. On April 15, 1962, Sartre wrote to Schweitzer of their mutual desire to help underdeveloped countries and to ban the bomb. "We often have the same aims without having the same principles, and that is the basis of a fruitful collaboration." He added, "Each time I see your name amongst those who fight against atomic warfare, I feel myself close to you."

Unlike Russell and Sartre, Schweitzer's opposition to nuclear bombs derived from his Christian convictions. Paradoxically, this same secure base in the piety of late-nineteenth-century Lutheranism had enabled him to take such risks in exploring the historicity of the accounts of Jesus that were part of his heritage. In 1958 he wrote to Marc Teuscher, a correspondent from Casablanca, "Since my youth I have been under the influence of pietism, and this enabled me to pursue my study of Jesus with total liberty." By contrast, others, he explained, had been unable to stomach the essentially eschatological aspects of the New Testament, while many theologians had simply ignored them.

Moreover, he added, he was also orthodox, since he demanded the abolition of atomic bombs, which the leaders of Catholicism and Protestantism had not sufficient spirit to condemn. Schweitzer took with utmost reverence the biblical injunction not to kill. It seemed to him more relevant than ever. In a lecture on atomic weapons and culture he noted how from the beginning of the twentieth century the range and explosive power of missiles had increased enormously. Shells launched from invisible submarines menaced ships, and cities were vulnerable from the air. It was no longer possible to distinguish between combatants and civilians, and he concluded that the attempts to humanize war in the name of morality, which had been begun by the seventeenth-century Dutch jurist Hugo Grotius, could no longer be sustained.

"The possession of power through atomic weapons is sinister indeed," said Schweitzer. "The potential of the latest atomic weapons is so overwhelming that they can in effect be no longer used to wage war. They cannot be used to conquer territory, nor are they suitable for attack." As for the so-called balance of atomic power, the result of this state of affairs was that both sides were engaged in an unending arms race, in which neither side could know for certain whether it was ahead of the other or had fallen behind. "A situation where both sides are re-arming cannot ensure peace," Schweitzer preached.

With regard to the ecological effects of atomic testing he was equally pessimistic: "Men and women drink radioactive water and radioactive milk, which comes from cows that have been fed on radioactive grass or hay. They eat fruit and vegetables which have become radioactive." In his view, "Atomic weapons have brought about an unexpected situation in which the will for power has become a will to renounce power." Schweitzer concluded on a spiritual note: Mankind needed to establish an atmosphere of mutual trust, and "the establishment of mutual trust is something spiritual, an ethical relationship between human beings and nations characterized by truthfulness and a deeply felt responsibility."

In private, Schweitzer was scathing about public figures who refused to condemn nuclear tests and nuclear weapons. On May 17, 1958, he told Norman Cousins, "Also the Pope we will leave alone. He is a great Sir, and he owes consideration to the church. He may be a good man but he is no fighter. Or did you read anywhere, that he condemned the atomic and H-Bombs in the name of Christian religion? Protestantism does it, but there is no Catholic declaration so far."

Incessantly Schweitzer badgered the political rulers of the world over this issue. During the crisis over Berlin in 1957 he was fairly sanguine, and told Norman Cousins in a letter of November 10 that he was certain that the diplomats would find a way out without recourse to war. For that reason, he said, he would remain silent, pronouncing only on matters of disarmament and peace. But the following year he was speaking at a rally in Berlin against the installation of missile bases in the Federal Republic of Germany. When the American scientist Dr. Linus Pauling organized a petition to the United Nations calling for an end to nuclear tests, Schweitzer's name appeared prominently among the rest. In the same year he made three broadcasts from Oslo, attacking such mirages as the idea of a "clean" bomb. "The clean hydrogen bomb is intended for window dressing, not for use," he declared. As for nuclear tests, "Mankind is imperiled by them," he said. "Mankind insists that they stop, and has every right to do."

In 1962, when President of the United States, John F. Kennedy, and his defense secretary, Robert S. McNamara, seemed willing to use nuclear weapons to keep the Russians out of Cuba, Schweitzer wrote an open letter to the latter, declaring that, "A war fought with atomic weapons is something so horrible that not even military people and the scientists concerned with the real significance of atomic weapons, can have a full notion about it." Quiet, positive negotiations, not war, would resolve such problems, he urged, for "the atomic war has nothing to do any more with two belligerent nations, but with the whole of humanity. He who decides for atomic war takes a terrible responsibility towards mankind. Nobody can release him from this responsibility."

In 1954, Schweitzer was awarded the Nobel Peace Prize for his work among lepers. With his flair for publicity, he announced that the prize had enabled him to build a corrugated iron roof for the leper colony that he had founded in 1952 just outside his Lambaréné hospital in memory of his mother and father. He used the rest of the money to install a radiography unit in the hospital. And he arrived in Europe accompanied by three chimpanzees that he intended to donate to the Paris zoo.

Just as long ago he had given away his university scholarship to the needy Jäger, so he was still impulsively generous. Learning in 1953 that the chapel of the Catholic mission in Lambaréné had no tiles for its roof, he gave Marie-Agnès, the sister in charge, tiles and hammers and lent her two workmen. As he put it, "The priest at the Catholic mission is your father *in spiritualibus* and as for me, I am your father *in temporalibus.*" His letter gave an account of Schweitzer's own leper hospital. In the last three years the work had become overwhelming, he wrote. Beginning with 250 lepers, his hospital had doubled in size, and his anxieties had doubled equally, "for in these unstable economic times it is extremely difficult to keep going an enterprise that has become too large."

He gratefully took the Nobel Prize money, and he used the opportunity once more to preach peace. Lecturing in the hall of Oslo University in the presence of King Haakon VII and Princess

Astrid, he declared, "It is my belief that one day we shall reach the point where we shall refrain from wars for moral reasons, because we feel that war is a crime against humanity." Schweitzer advanced the paradox that the more we become supermen (by, for example, learning how to fly), the more we become inhuman. "The horror of this experience must arouse us out of our stupor, so that we can direct our wills and our hopes toward the coming of an era in which there will no longer be wars."

Hélène was present at Oslo, having first refused to come if one of Schweitzer's aides, a pastor's widow named Emmy Martin who had been close to him ever since she persuaded Beck Verlag to publish his *Philosophy of Civilisation*, also came. Rhena even wrote to her father that Hélène was threatening to divorce him. In the event, Schweitzer's wife arrived and sat beside him, speaking not a word. Hélène by now deeply resented the women who worked in Lambaréné alongside her husband, where she would have been but for her illness, women such as the imperious leper nurse Trudi Bochsler; Mathilde Kottmann who had been at Lambaréné since the 1920s; his extremely beautiful senior nurse, the Dutchwoman Alida Silver, who had arrived just after World War II; and her urbane and witty fellow countrywoman Tony van Leer. Undoubtedly Hélène resented the free-and-easy relationships of the jungle hospital. Schweitzer never minded if some of his doctors and nurses formed romantic attachments in his jungle hospital. After all, they were young men and women set together in remarkable intimacy. Secondly, Schweitzer himself clearly relished the company of these women, as they relished him. An American visitor, Norman Cousins, overheard them planning a party for Schweitzer in his eighty-first year. "We will wear our dresses for dinner," they agreed. "And we will do our hair specially." When Schweitzer appeared some of them had ribbons in their hair and others were wearing lipstick. The doctor responded in kind, producing a bottle of fine burgundy from a case someone had recently sent him. Then he told a story of how, at the age of sixteen, he and a cousin had lied to their grandfather, pretending to be visiting a relative when in reality they were setting off for a beer tavern. Ten minutes later their grandfather arrived at the same tavern. "An old man isn't as blind as you might think," he observed. "And sometimes he's just as thirsty as younger men." So he ordered his grandsons to pour him a drink. At the end of the tale Schweitzer turned to his American visitor with the remark, "I'd better be careful, or Mr. Cousins will think I do nothing except tell funny stories." And Cousins later wrote, "The dining-room was transformed into a small banquet hall and young ladies, gay and lovely, adorned the table."

This was the company from which Schweitzer's wife had long been excluded. But when Schweitzer quitted Europe for the penultimate time in 1955, Hélène soon joined him. Sitting behind him, she was photographed, both of them holding solar topees, their dog at their feet. By Hélène's leg is a bamboo rod. Norman Cousins, who visited Lambaréné shortly before her husband's eighty-second birthday, recalled that she used it to fend off some of the animals, including a particularly obtrusive bird that was half raven, half parrot which otherwise disturbed her rest. "Mrs. Schweitzer liked to doze in her chair," he recalled. "So long as she held onto the bamboo rod, the bird respected her solitude." As soon as the rod was absent, he would flap down onto her shoulder.

Cousins could see that Hélène was ill. "The blue veins stood out in her forehead and seemed stark against the pure whiteness of her skin," he wrote. "She had lovely gray-brown eyes but they seemed to look at you through a mist. She spoke with difficulty, and her breathing was labored." Even with the aid of a stick she found it hard to negotiate the two dozen steps across the compound and climb up to the dining room. Once Cousins saw her start out, bent forward over her stick, and rushed to help her, but she smiled, thanked him, and said she was in the habit of getting around by herself. "It makes me feel so foolish, this being so helpless," she told him. "I ought to be working with the doctor. He is an amazing man. I really think he is working harder now than he did twenty years ago. And twenty years ago I was afraid he was killing himself with work."

Soon the oppressive heat proved more than Hélène

Schweitzer could bear. In May 1957, Tony van Leer took her back to Europe. Ten days later she died in a Zurich clinic. Albert reached Europe three months afterward, driven around by one of his devoted lady friends (this time Erica Anderson). He presented the Königsfeld home to the Moravians. And on Christmas Day he was back in Lambaréné, bringing the ashes of his wife, which were buried outside his study window in a plot marked by a cross carved by Schweitzer himself.

Rhena had joined him, working as a pathologist in the hospital. Schweitzer was now a vegetarian, living almost entirely on lentil soup. Ali Silver had taken to sleeping in a hammock in his room, in case he needed medical help during the night. Occasionally, he would forget things, but otherwise he seemed well. Then, on August 23, 1965, he startled his fellow workers by announcing the arrangements for his death. The following Friday he walked through his orchard, saying good-bye to each individual tree.

Ali Silver linked his arm and took him back to his room. She urged him to write to one of his correspondents, but the pen fell from his hand. On September 4 at 11:30 in the evening, Albert Schweitzer died. "If you study life deeply, looking perceptively into the vast and animated chaos that is creation, the profundity of it all will stun you," he had preached in February 1919. "You will recognize yourself in everything. That tiny beetle which lies dead in your path was a living creature, struggling like you for existence, rejoicing like you in the warmth of the sun, like you knowing fear and pain. Now it is no more than decaying matter, as you too sooner or later will be."

A couple of months later, on December 23, 1965, Mrs. Oberman, one of the Dutch workers at the hospital, wrote to George Marshall, "One morning I awoke at six o'clock to the singing of children and adults." They sang for half an hour, expressing their love and gratitude for Schweitzer. "It moved me thoroughly, and I thought of the doctor, how this would touch him in his soul." Then she added, "Once a native said to him, when you die we will have a tom-tom of a week to mourn you. The doctor replied, 'fortunately I won't hear it.'"

Select Bibliography

Bauer, Walter. *Heinrich Julius Holtzmann*. Alfred Töpelmann, Giessen 1932.

Bibliothèque Nationale et Universitaire, Strasbourg. *Albert Schweitzer 1875–1975*. (exhibition catalogue) 1985.

Brabazon, James. *Albert Schweitzer: A Comprehensive Biography*. London: Victor Gollancz, 1976.

Budde, Karl Ferdinand Reinhardt. *The Religion of Israel to the Exile*. New York: G. P. Putnam's Sons, 1899.

Colani, Timothée. *Jésus-Christ et les croyances messianiques de son temps*. Strasbourg: G. Silbermann, 1864.

"Colloque A. Schweitzer." *Revue d'Histoire et de Philosophie Religieuses* 56: (1–2). Paris: Presses Universitaires de France, 1976.

Correspondence of Noel Gillespie, 1922–52. *Wisconsin Magazine of History* 54 (1971).

Cousins, Norman. *Albert Schweitzer's Mission: Healing and Peace*. New York: W. W. Norton and Company, 1985.

Cousins, Norman. *Dr. Schweitzer of Lambaréné*. London: A & C Black, 1960.

Dupré, Marcel. *Marcel Dupré raconte*. Paris: Éditions Bornemann, 1972.

Gräuer, Erich. *Albert Schweitzer als Theologe*. Tübingen, Germany: J. C. B. Mohr (Paul Siebeck), 1979.

Groos, Helmut. *Albert Schweitzer. Grösse und Grenzen—Eine kritische Würdigung des Forschers und Denkers*. Munich: E. Reinhardt, 1974.

von Harnack, Adolf. *Das apostolische Glaubensbekenntnis: Ein geschichtlicher Bericht nebst einem Nachwort*. Berlin: A. Haack, 1892.

—."Das doppelte Evangelium in dem Neuen Testament" (1910). *Aus Wissenschaft und Leben* II. Giessen: Alfred Töpelmann, 1911.

—."Was hat die Historie an fester Erkenntnis zur Deutung des Weltgeschehens zu bieten?" *Ausgewählte Reden und Aufsätze*. Berlin: W. de Gruyten, 1951.

Holtzmann, H. J. *Die synoptischen Evangelien, ihr Ursprung und geschichtlicher Charakter*. Leipzig: Wilhelm Engelmann, 1863.

Huard, P. "Albert Schweitzer l'africain (1875–1965)." *Le Concours Médical*, 88 (ler janvier, 1966).

International Albert Schweitzer Symposium. *Report on the International Albert Schweitzer Symposium*, 28 September–1 October 1978, Deventer, Holland, 1978.

"Karl Budde." *Journal of Biblical Literature* 55 (1936).

Kümmel, W. G. *The New Testament: The History of its Investigation and its Problems*. London: Penguin Books, 1972.

Loesche, G. *Johannes Mathesius. Ein Lebens und Sitten-Bild aus der Reformationzeit*. Gotha: F. A. Perthes, 1895.

Marshall, George, and David Poling. *Schweitzer*. New York: Doubleday & Co., 1971.

Mathesius, Johannes. *Ausgewählte Werke*, vols. 1–4. Edited with an introduction and commentary by G. Loesche. Prague: G. Freytag, 1896–1908.

McKnight, Gerald. *Verdict on Schweitzer*. London: Frederick Muller, 1964.

Micklem, Nathaniel. *The Box and the Puppets*. London: Geoffrey Bles, 1957.

Oswald, Suzanne. *Mein Onkel Bery. Erinnerungen an Albert Schweitzer*. Zürich: Rotapfel-Verlag, 1980.

Pierhal, Jean. *Albert Schweitzer: Das Leben eines guten Menschen*. Munich: Kindler Verlag, 1957.

Radhakrishnan, Sarvepalli. *Eastern Religions and Western Thought*. Oxford: Clarendon Press, 1939.

Roback, A. A., ed. *In Albert Schweitzer's Realms: A Symposium*. Cambridge, Mass.: Sci-Art Publishers, 1962.

Sartre, Jean-Paul. *Les Mots, Et Words*. Irene Clephane, translator. London: Hamish Hamilton, 1964.

Schweitzer, Charles. *Méthode directe pour l'enseignement de la langue française*. Paris: A. Colin, 1920.

Seaver, George. *Albert Schweitzer: The Man and his Mind*. London: Adam and Charles Black, 1947.

Woytt-Secretan, Marie. *Albert Schweitzer construit l'Hôspital de Lambaréné*. Paris-Strasbourg: Editions Oberlin, 1959.

von Zahn-Harnack, Agnes. *Adolf von Harnack*. Berlin: H. Bott, 1951.

Index

204 / Index

208 / *Index*